GW01221022

Korean Religious Texts in Iconic and Performative Rituals

Comparative Research on Iconic and Performative Texts

Series Editor: James W. Watts, Syracuse University

While humanistic scholarship has focused on the semantic meaning of written, printed, and electronic texts, it has neglected how people perform texts mentally, orally and theatrically and manipulate the material text through aesthetic engagement, ritual display, and physical decoration. Ritualizing the material form of books — their iconic dimension — is to revere them as objects of power rather than just as words of instruction, information, or insight. Ritualizing books' expressive or performative dimension through song, artistic illustration and theater aims for inspirational effects.

This series encourages innovative research on the iconic and expressive/performative uses of written texts. It supports the activities of the Society for Comparative Research on Iconic and Performative Texts (SCRIPT), and also studies of these issues by other groups and individual scholars.

PUBLISHED

Books as Bodies and as Sacred Beings
Edited by James W. Watts and Yohan Yoo

How and Why Books Matter: Essays on the Social Function of Iconic Texts
James W. Watts

Iconic Books and Texts
Edited by James W. Watts

Miniature Books: The Format and Function of Tiny Religious Texts
Edited by Kristina Myrvold and Dorina Miller Parmenter

Reframing Authority: The Role of Media and Materiality
Edited by Laura Feldt and Christian Hogel

Sensing Sacred Texts
Edited by James W. Watts

Korean Religious Texts in Iconic and Performative Rituals

Yohan Yoo

equinox

SHEFFIELD UK   BRISTOL CT

Published by Equinox Publishing Ltd.
UK: Office 415, The Workstation, 15 Paternoster Row, Sheffield, South Yorkshire, S1 2BX
USA: ISD, 70 Enterprise Drive, Bristol, CT 06010

www.equinoxpub.com

First published 2024
© Yohan Yoo 2024.

All rights reserved. No part of this publication may be reproduced or transmitted in any form or by any means, electronic or mechanical, including photocopying, recording or any information storage or retrieval system, without prior permission in writing from the publishers.

British Library Cataloguing-in-Publication Data

A catalogue record for this book is available from the British Library.

ISBN-13 978 1 80050 496 7 (hardback)
978 1 80050 497 4 (paperback)
978 1 80050 498 1 (epdf)
978 1 80050 615 2 ePub

Library of Congress Cataloging-in-Publication Data

Names: Yu, Yo-han, 1971- author.
Title: Korean religious texts in iconic and performative rituals / Yohan Yoo.
Description: Sheffield, South Yorkshire : Equinox Publishing Ltd., 2024. | Series: Comparative research on iconic and performative texts | Includes bibliographical references and index. | Summary: "This book examines the ways in which scriptures are accepted and appropriated by religious people in Korea. It explores how sacred texts in various religions, including Protestantism, Buddhism, Confucianism, and Shamanism, attain their sacred status and power. It also delves into how the performative aspect of scriptures is often intrinsically linked to their iconic status"— Provided by publisher.
Identifiers: LCCN 2024017376 (print) | LCCN 2024017377 (ebook) | ISBN 9781800504967 (hardback) | ISBN 9781800504974 (paperback) | ISBN 9781800504981 (ePDF) | ISBN 9781800506152 (ePub)
Subjects: LCSH: Korea—Religion. | Sacred books—History and criticism. | Ritual—Korea—History.
Classification: LCC BL2231 .Y89 2024 (print) | LCC BL2231 (ebook) | DDC 322/.109519—dc23/eng/20240726
LC record available at https://lccn.loc.gov/2024017376
LC ebook record available at https://lccn.loc.gov/2024017377

Edited and Typeset by Queenston Publishing, Hamilton Canada.

Contents

List of Figures	vi
Preface and Acknowledgements	vii
1. Introduction: Explaining Sacred Texts and Religion by Using Korean Examples	1
2. Possession and Repetition: How Korean Lay Buddhists Appropriate Scriptures	27
3. Performative Scripture Reading Rituals in Early Korean Protestantism	43
4. Sensory Readings of Scriptures by Neo-Confucian Scholars	59
5. Performing Scriptures: Ritualizing Sacred Texts in Korean Shamanic Recitation of Scriptures	69
6. Powerful Tiny Scriptures: Miniature Sutras in Korean Buddhism	85
7. Scriptures for Recitation in Donghak (Eastern Learning)	99
Bibliography	125
Index	135

List of Figures

2.1	*Yunjangdae* in Yongmunsa temple, Yecheon, Korea.	36
2.2	*Haeindo* in Haeinsa temple, Hapcheon, Korea.	38
5.1	*Seolwi*, making or installing paper figures and banners.	77
5.2	A *gyeonggaek* reciting scriptures while remaining seated in a local festival.	77
5.3	*Seolwis* reflecting the contents of scriptures.	82
5.4	*Seolwis* reflecting the contents of scriptures.	82
6.1	Miniature sutras and readable mini-sutras.	91
6.2	A miniature sutra in hand.	91
6.3	Items including miniature sutras that are stored in domestic small Buddha statues.	93
6.4	Inserting the box that includes miniature sutras into a small Buddha statue.	93
6.5	*Hosinyong* miniature sutras carried in purses or bags.	94
6.6	Miniature sutras for key chains or cellphones.	96
6.7	A plastic box miniature sutra with a hole into which a paper scroll sutra is inserted.	96
7.1	The contents page of the 1883 edition of *Donggyeongdaejeon*.	101
7.2	Yongdam pavilion rebuilt in 1975 by Cheondogyo. The area surrounding this building is a holy site for Cheondogyo.	103
7.3	"Jeopryeongganghwado," a print included in the *Sicheongyojoyujeokdoji*	112

PREFACE AND ACKNOWLEDGMENTS

This book owes enormous and long-term debts to my graduate advisor, Professor James W. Watts. In the first semester of my graduate study at Syracuse University, which was fall 2001, I took Professor Watts' graduate seminar titled "Sacrifice." Because he was a scholar of the Hebrew Bible, I first thought that I would be mainly required to read parts on sacrificial ritual in *Leviticus* and other books of Pentateuch, but my guess turned out wrong. It was a seminar of comparative religion referring to sacrificial rituals. We read and thought about important ritual theories from the classical one of William Robertson Smith to Nancy Jay's feminist perspective, while scrutinizing various cases from diverse religious traditions. Professor Watts was, and still is, an exemplary scholar of comparative religion, as well as a great scholar of the Hebrew Bible. In his graduate seminar on scripture, I learned that we should consider non-semantic aspects of the religious texts, such as expressive and materialistic ones, to understand how religious people regard, adopt, and appropriate them. It is thanks to Professor Watts that I could foster a broader understanding of scripture and conduct research on iconic and performative aspects of sacred texts in Korean religions. He was my teacher and is now the most reliable colleague of mine, with whom I co-authored *Cosmologies of Pure Realms and the Rhetoric of Pollution* (Routledge, 2021) and co-edited *Books as Bodies and as Sacred Beings* (Equinox, 2021). Therefore, I dedicate this book to Professor Watts.

Through Professor Watts, I joined the Society of Comparative Research on Iconic and Performative Texts (SCRIPT), which he co-founded with S. Brent Plate and Dorina Miller Parmenter in 2010. My research that adds up to this book was possible thanks to the academic influence of colleagues of this society. I was fortunate enough to meet good colleagues in SCRIPT, among whom I would like to express my special thanks to S. Brent Plate, one of the co-founders and the first president of the society, for the collaboration and friendship I have had with him. I was given the opportunity to develop ideas on sacred texts of Korean religions in the second and the third Iconic Books Symposia, held at Hamilton College in 2009 and Syracuse University in 2010. I received helpful responses, comments, and stimuli from great scholars who participated in the symposia, such as William Graham who was surprisingly erudite on various religious traditions with proficiency in their languages, Laurie Patton who gave me a very powerful but modest encouragement to stick to my own thesis more strongly, and Vincent Wimbush thanks to whom I could recognize the power of scripture in the lives of religious people more clearly. Since then, I have had chances to present papers at several SCRIPT panels of the annual meetings of AAR/SBL (2011, 2013, 2017), at a symposium that took place at Ruhr University in Bochum, Germany in 2016 on the theme "Seeing, Touching, Holding and Tasting Sacred Texts," and at a conference at Seoul National University in 2017 on the topic "Books as Sacred Beings."

Five chapters of this book were presented at those conferences and published in *Postscripts*, the official journal of SCRIPT, and have been revised and updated for inclusion here. Chapter 2 "Possession and Repetition" is a revised version of "Possession and Repetition: Ways in which Korean Lay Buddhists Appropriate Scriptures," *Postscripts* 6 (2010 [2012]),[1] 243–259, reprinted in *Iconic Books and Texts* (ed. Watts; Sheffield: Equinox, 2013), 299–313. An earlier version of Chapter 3 "Performative Scripture Reading Ritual" first appeared as "Public Scripture Reading Rituals in Early Korean Protestantism," in *Postscripts* 2 (2006 [2008]), 226–240. Chapter 4 "Sensory Readings of Scriptures" first appeared as "Neo-Confucian Sensory Readings of Scriptures: The Reading of Methods of Chu Hsi and Yi Hwang," in *Postscripts* 8 (2012 [2017]), 161–172, reprinted in *Sensing Sacred Texts* (ed. Watts; Sheffield: Equinox, 2018), 161–172. Chapter 5 "Performing Scriptures" first appeared as "Performing Scriptures: Ritualizing Written Texts in *Seolwi-Seolgyeong*, the Korean Shamanistic Recitation of Scriptures," in *Postscripts* 10 (2019), 9–25, reprinted in *Books as Bodies and as Sacred Beings* (eds. Watts and Yoo; Sheffield: Equinox, 2021), 9–24. Chapter 6 "Powerful Tiny Scriptures" was first published as "Sutras Working in Buddha's Belly and Buddhists' Pockets: Miniature Sutras in Korean Buddhism," in *Postscripts* 9 (2013 [2018]), 269–284, reprinted in *Miniature Books: The Format and Function of Tiny Religious Text* (eds. Kristina Myrvold and Dorina Miller Parmenter; Sheffield: Equinox, 2019), 201–215. Chapter 6 was co-authored with Professor Emeritus Woncheol Yun, Seoul National University. I thank

---

1. References to *Postscripts* are dated as follows: cover date [publication date].

Preface and Acknowledgments

Professor Yun, who is one of my best friends now, but was first my teacher and senior colleague, for his permission to include the chapter in this volume. I am grateful to Janet Joyce of Equinox Publishing for agreeing to the republication in this book. Chapter 7 "Scriptures for Recitation," which has not been published previously, was supposed to be presented at the annual meeting of AAR in 2020 under the title of "Recitation of Scriptures in Donghak (Eastern Learning), a Korean Religion Founded in the mid-19th century," but that year's SCRIPT panel was cancelled due to COVID-19. I finally completed this chapter in the spring of 2023, which I added to this volume. I have also added a comprehensive and comparative introductory chapter in which I clarify some theoretical and methodological issues with studying religion and religious texts.

To demonstrate some general characteristics of sacred texts on the basis of Korean examples to students of religion in as many countries or regions as possible, I have written this volume in English, which is broadly accepted as the language of academics. But they were written by a Korean scholar, who thinks, speaks, writes, and teaches in the Korean language. To communicate with most students of religion in the contemporary world, I have had to write in English which is not my language. I have been doing this work for "the disquieting, challenging work of critical encounter" without which "scholarship cannot continue," according to Kathryn Lofton. As she properly points out, "Universities require scholarship, yes, but even more than that they need conversation; they need listening" (Lofton 2017, 290). To make academic conversation with as many scholars of religion in the world as possible, to let them listen to what a Korean scholar says, and to listen to what they think about my work, I chose to present and write in English. Of course, I have published many more papers and books in Korean than in English, not only for my fellow Korean readers but also for myself, because writing in Korean is a lot easier for me. My colleagues from English speaking countries do not know how much sweat I was soaked in so as to write just one sentence or even to select a word, being busy in consulting dictionaries. But I decided to participate in academic conversation with scholars of religion around the world by gathering and showing Korean cases, which I believe will be useful for developing explanatory models that can be applied to many cultures and regions besides Korea. It was for the sake of this conversation that I had to cope with dripping sweat when I wrote in English.

However, I am also aware that more pains may be taken by the readers of my English writings. I think my colleagues whose first language is English must have had difficulty trying to understand my presentations and writings in English. I would like to thank my colleagues in US, especially those of SCRIPT, for their patience in endeavoring to understand my awkward spoken and written English. They may be surprised to see that I can express myself very fluently in Korean, freely employing fancy words and powerful rhetoric, which is an ability I have never been able to show them in English. I did my best to make sentences and paragraphs of this book that are easily understandable, giving up impressive writing. But many confusing words and phrases in this book may bother some readers, for which I am responsible. English translations of Korean and Classical Chinese quotations in this book are mine, unless otherwise indicated. I basically tried to have my translations make sense to readers from English speaking countries rather than making literal translations. I am to blame for any mistakes that may be found in this book. For transliterations of Korean words into Roman letters, I follow the transcription system established by the National Institute of the Korean Language.

My research for this book has benefited from the support of Seoul National University (SNU). SNU not only has always generously supported my participation in conferences abroad, without which this book could not be completed, but also provided a grant for the SCRIPT conference at SNU in 2017. Without the tremendous help of my colleagues at SNU, this book would not be possible. I will mention here just some of my colleagues in the Department of Religious Studies and the College of Humanities at SNU. However, I would like to make it clear that I am grateful to all faculty members in my department, including professors and lecturers, for their solid support for my research. If it had not been for the constant encouragement of Professor Emeritus Chongsuh Kim, my undergraduate advisor, I would not have decided to pursue my graduate degrees in religious studies. Professor Emeritus Woncheol Yun, the co-author of the original version of Chapter 6, gave very productive comments on Chapter 2 also. I received great assistance from Professor Jongseong Choi to collect data for supporting my arguments in Chapters 5 and 7. Doctor Booyeon Lim spared no pains in helping me read Confucian materials written in classical Chinese while I prepared the original version of Chapter 4. Doctor Byoung Hoon Park, who is a specialist of Donghak *gasa*, meticulously read Chapter 7 and gave me useful advice. Professor Juhyung Rhi of the Department of Archeology and Art History helped me develop my points in Chapters 4 and 6. Graduate students of my department were willing to be the first readers of my papers. I am grateful to them for their questions and comments that were always helpful for elaborating my ideas. It is reassuring to have wonderful colleagues like them who tread together the path of studying religion.

Preface and Acknowledgments

When I endeavored to complete this book at its final stage during the spring and summer of 2023, which was the second half of my sabbatical year, the Institutes of Green Bio Science and Technology of SNU offered me an office and an apartment at Pyeongchang Campus, where I could concentrate on writing new chapters and revising published ones. At the breathtakingly beautiful and unbelievably noise-free Pyeongchang Campus of SNU, I could polish my ideas and expressions. How blessed I am to be a professor who studies and teaches at SNU!

1

INTRODUCTION:
EXPLAINING SACRED TEXTS AND RELIGION BY USING KOREAN EXAMPLES

Comparative research conducted by a Korean scholar

Most studies on scripture have focused on the contents of the text, that is, its semantic dimension. However, the text's contents often do not play a critical role in the lives of many religious people, as is revealed in cases of so-called pre-modern religions, most of whose adherents could not read or write. Research putting undue value on the contents is likely to miss the role and significance of scriptures in the lives of such people. Wilfred Cantwell Smith already in 1971 showed concern about this problem and pointed out that scholars of religion should pay attention to the roles that scripture plays in the life of religious people (W. C. Smith 1971). It was around the beginning of the new millennium that scholars got down to studying other aspects of scripture rather than only its contents. James W. Watts made a significant contribution to this change of focus by emphasizing the importance of the iconic dimension of scripture, which has to do with the sacred status of the physical text, and the performative dimension, which is ritualized by performing the text or its contents. To explain non-semantic aspects of scriptures, a group of scholars, including Watts, founded the Society for Comparative Research on Iconic and Performative Texts (SCRIPT) in 2010. I have had many chances to participate in SCRIPT and have presented five papers focusing on sacred texts of Korean religions in the meetings of the society. In those five papers, which were later published in the official journal of the society, *Postscripts*, I tried to articulate how the sacred status of scriptures are attained and their power exercised by investigating how scriptures are accepted and appropriated by religious people in Korea. In my own estimation, examples of Korean religions, including Protestantism, Buddhism, Confucianism, and Shamanism, turn out to be very useful for showing non-semantic aspects of sacred texts, especially in demonstrating how scriptures are performed and how the performative dimension of scriptures is inseparably related to their iconic status. Therefore, I decided to collect together and revise these published chapters in this volume, along with a newly written Chapter 7, which focuses on the recitation of scriptures of Donghak, a Korean religion founded in the mid-nineteenth century.

While Korean people have a shared linguistic, historical, and cultural background for a very long time, different religions coexist in a peculiar state of balance in Korea. That is one of the reasons examples from Korea are helpful in demonstrating the way religious people in general recognize and appropriate sacred texts, as well as the way those who belong to a specific religious group do so. For readers who do not know the religious situation of Korea, I will briefly introduce the present religious topography. Though Christianity is the largest religion in South Korea, accounting for 27.7% of the population according to the November 2015 census, Buddhism occupies 15.5% of the population and exercises no less influence than Christianity by taking the position of the only major *jeontongjonggyo* (traditional religion) of Korea. Furthermore, Confucianism, which not only was the official ideology of elite scholars, but also provided a predominant worldview and way of life for most Koreans during the Joseon Dynasty (1392–1910), remains influential in the form of ancestral rites and in the custom of giving precedence to elders. Many contemporary Koreans also still rely on shamanic rituals and divination, which have prevailed among the common people for thousands of years. In addition, many new religious movements have appeared in Korea since the late nineteenth century and some of them were or are prevalent. The first among the new religions of Korea is Donghak (Eastern Learning), which was founded in 1860. The following chapters cover examples from Buddhism, Christianity, Confucianism, shamanism, and Donghak.

I am confident that examples from Korean religions can do much for developing comparative perspectives on religious texts. Discussing religions in Korea is in practice dealing with many of the so-called "religions of the world." By observing religions in Korea, it is possible to develop more general theories and explanations. Besides, this mix of religions allows Koreans to see clearly what is often missed by others. This is similar to Romania as described by Mircea Eliade. Eliade said that the culture of his homeland Romania "formed a sort of bridge between the West and Byzantium, while also linking the Slavic world with the Oriental world and the Mediterranean world" (Eliade 1982, 16). Politically, the position of his homeland helped him understand the repressed situation of colonized India. Though he recognized Romania as "a country that had never had any

Explaining Sacred Texts and Religion by Using Korean Examples

colonies" and "that had in fact been treated like a colony itself for centuries," he also said that his homeland is a European country and he himself was a white European (Eliade 1982, 53). Thanks to this bridge position of his homeland, he could be more sensitive than those from England or France to the repression and injustice he witnessed in India. Eliade also said that he could take advantage of his heritage as a Romanian and easily understand both customs that were "inherited from Rome" and those that were "influenced by the East and rooted in the Neolithic era" (Eliade 1982, 98).

I argue that Korea is indeed "a sort of bridge" in the present-day world, between the West and the East, the modern and the pre-modern, and in a sense, the future and the past. South Korea currently enjoys great economic and cultural prosperity, yet many people in the northern half of the peninsula live in distress under dictatorship. While Korea is known to have developed so-called futuristic technology at a very high level, most Korean people still remember the tragic experiences of the colonial period (1910-1945). In other words, though Korea is now one of the most modern countries, it was an extremely poor, colonized country less than a century ago. Above all, we should consider the religious topography of Korea. Christianity, which is the representative Western religion, and Buddhism, which is regarded as a traditional religion, maintain the balance of power. In a country where the cutting-edge technology of artificial intelligence and new renewable energy is rapidly developing, the influence of Confucianism and shamanism is still conspicuous.

I think examples from this country that is in the position of a bridge can be applied more broadly. Remarkable religions of the world gather together in this bridge country under the title of Korean religions, strongly influencing the society and people living in it. By investigating the religions of Korea, a scholar can cover these multiple religions. Just remember that chapters of this book range from Buddhism, Christianity, Confucianism, and shamanism to a newly founded Korean religion, which correspond to about half of so the called "world religions" along with a new religious movement. These examples work together to demonstrate how the iconic and performative dimensions of sacred texts are ritualized by religious people. It is possible to demonstrate rather general features of sacred texts by dealing with examples from the religions of Korea.

The bridge position of Korea, between traditional and Western religions, modern and pre-modern, future and past, surely have exercised great influence on me, the author of this book. I think I myself can and should play the role of the bridge in academia: while I was born and have spent most of my life in Korea, I received my graduate degrees in an institution of the United States. I am a Korean who cherishes the sentiments, emotions, and traditional ways of thinking which are shared by most Koreans, but at the same time, I was born into a Christian family and have lived as a Christian. As a Korean scholar of comparative religion, who is not only acquainted with characteristics of the modern scholarship that has been systemized in the West, but also is able to see some aspects of religions that are difficult for Western scholars to approach, I hope to unravel what some Western scholars often overlook. The religious history and topography of Korea will help reveal dots that Western scholars miss while painting a picture of religion.

I hope readers of this book will be persuaded that the views of a scholar of religion who is in the bridge position can be helpful to discern and explain more than one dimension or more than one aspectual characteristic of religion which are inseparably comingled. Expressions of subtraction, like "not A but B" or "B rather than A," which some Western scholars habitually and obsessively resort to, are sometimes not appropriate for explaining an aspect of religion which is mixed with other aspects in extremely intricate ways. Multiple dimensions are in many cases comingled in the lives of religious people, and specifically for the theme of this book, in how they adopt, regard, and appropriate sacred texts. Expressions of addition, like "A and at once B," "A as well as B," or "A along with B" should be used more often, which I will try to do in this book.

I would like to emphasize that this book is the research outcome of a comparative study of religion. It is true that each chapter pays attention to one specific Korean religious tradition to demonstrate how religious people in Korea have recognized and appropriated the sacred status and power of scriptures. I do not try to draw a full-scale comparison between the specific tradition and another example from different traditions in each chapter. However, it is also true that this book covers multiple religious traditions on the particular topic of iconic and performative scripture. Readers will see that I constantly compare the main topic with cases from other religions or cultures to make my explanation more persuasive. For example, in Chapter 3 public scripture reading rituals of Korean Protestant churches and African healing rituals are compared, clarifying similarities in performative utterances in the ritual context as well as many differences. In Chapter 5, I compare materialization of shamanic scriptures of the Chungcheong area with those of other areas including the Jeju province, pointing out that scriptures of the former, at least originally, existed in book form, while others existed and were transmitted only orally. In Chapter 7, I describe similarities and differences between the recitation

Explaining Sacred Texts and Religion by Using Korean Examples

of scriptures done by the intellectual elite and those done by the general public. In addition, while each chapter deals with the ritualization of sacred texts witnessed in different specific religions, the whole book includes various examples from multiple religions which altogether demonstrate ritualization of religious texts in general. Finally, chapters of this book are a part of larger comparative projects that invite multiple cases from various traditions on the iconic and performative scripture. This book is comparative in that it is composed of responses to invitations to engage in these comparative projects and it again invites more comparative works.

I am aware that examples of Korean religions may not be conclusive evidence proving that the iconic and the performative dimensions of scriptures are generally witnessed in most, if not all, religions that recognize scriptures. It is true that my chapters may be small dots of a picture painted by using the method of pointillism, but they will constitute important parts of a whole picture that reveals non-semantic aspects of sacred texts. My colleagues in SCRIPT have marked many dots and I expect more and more dots to be added by them. More pictures will be created and completed by way of pointillism, which is the way comparative scholarship should proceed according to Wendy Doniger (Doniger 2000, 70).

To the readers who expect broad and inclusive descriptions of sacred texts in Korea, this book may not be satisfactory because it limits its focus to the religious texts in iconic and performative ritual context. However, as Jonathan Z. Smith pointed out, comparative study of religion begins by limiting the focus of the data to a specific "aspectual characteristic" (Smith 1990, 53). This book will stick firmly to the aspectual characteristics it aims to articulate, which are how scriptures are accepted and used in Korea, how the sacred status of scriptures is attained and their power is exercised, and how the multiple dimensions of scriptures influence each other and function complementarily in the lives of religious people. It will be demonstrated that religious people in Korea have ritualized the contents of sacred texts in various forms, such as the published physical books, sounds from reading them aloud, letters written in them, and images made from them, in order to exert sacred power.

Eventually, I am sure that the topics this book focuses on will contribute to the broader understanding of more general characteristics of scriptures. My examples from Korean religions are dots of pointillism, which allude to the outline of the whole picture and make the outline visible and noticeable. Please be reminded that examples of Korean religions in this book include Buddhism, Christianity, Confucianism, shamanism, and a newly founded Korean religion in the nineteenth century, crossing ancient and modern ideas and practices, and crossing those that originated from the East and the West. Korean examples will prove that the iconic and the performative dimensions of scripture are witnessed in Korean religions and beyond. Korean religions will also show that the semantic and the non-semantic dimensions of scriptures influence each other and function complementarily in the lives of Korean religious people and those beyond Korea.

Readers of this book will see vivid examples from Korea and they will come to think that the aspectual characteristics found in Korea can also exist in other regions, times, and cultures, or can even be more generally witnessed. Many more dots are being added now, and will continue to be added, by my colleagues in SCRIPT to complete the picture of iconic and performative scripture.

Using and extending the new model of three dimensions of scriptures

I hope that the title of this book, *Korean Religious Texts in Iconic and Performative Rituals*, reflects clearly what I want to show. I think the scope of data I deal with is revealed quite well by the phrase "Korean Religious Texts," which I use as a concise expression for written and oral texts whose sacred authority is recognized by religious communities in Korea. I should explain what I mean by 'ritual,' the last word of the title. I accept one of the widely known definitions of ritual "as those conscious and voluntary, repetitious and stylized symbolic bodily actions that are centered on cosmic structures and/or sacred presences" (Zuesse 2005, 7834). For the theme of this book, however, this term should be applied more specifically, so as to highlight what religious people do with sacred texts. For this purpose, I would like to argue that for "conscious and voluntary, repetitious and stylized symbolic bodily actions" to be centered on sacred presences or powers, the object that is to be accepted as sacred should be differentiated from others. It is what ritual is, as well as what ritual does, as Jonathan Z. Smith avers "Ritual is, above all, an assertion of difference" (Smith 1987, 109). Based on this definition of ritual by Smith and his other explanations of it, Watts goes further and argues that "the religious adoption and use of scriptures should be understood as a form of ritual" (Watts 2006 [2008], 140). According to Smith, "ritual relies for its power on the fact that it is concerned with quite ordinary activities placed within an extraordinary setting, that what it describes and displaces, is, in principle, possible for every occurrence of these acts" (Smith 1987, 109). In this sense, Watts points out that even textual interpretation should be considered a form of ritual, because the practice of academic interpretation pays "detailed attention to ordinary activities" (Watts 2006 [2008], 144, fn5).

Explaining Sacred Texts and Religion by Using Korean Examples

In addition, I must also elucidate what I mean by "ritualization of scripture." In this book, following Watts's usage of the term, it designates what happens when religious groups regard, adopt, and appropriate sacred texts. If a person asserts the difference of a sacred book by interpreting, dramatizing, or decorating it, he or she is ritualizing the book. Ritualization is usually used to describe certain social actions that distinguish and privilege themselves in comparison to other actions (Bell 1992, 74, 88–93). According to Catherine Bell, "ritualization is a matter of various culturally specific strategies for setting some activities off from others, for creating and privileging a qualitative distinction between 'sacred' and 'profane,' and for ascribing such distinctions to realities thought to transcend the powers of human actors" (Bell 1992, 74). Ritualized acts are differentiated as more important or powerful and often have a dominant status (Bell 1992, 90). Though scriptures themselves are not actions or activities, they are objects differentiated by ritual activities and sometimes their presence makes ritual activities effective. Therefore, as Watts persuasively showed (Watts 2006 [2008]; Watts 2017, 257–260, 266), it can be said that scriptures are ritualized.

For the notions of the two important adjectives included in the title, "iconic" and "performative," I again rely on Watts's ideas about them. Watts has shown that "religious communities ritualize scriptures along three different dimensions: a semantic dimension, a performative dimension, and an iconic dimension" (Watts 2006 [2008], 140). The semantic dimension, which scholars have paid most attention to, has to do with scriptures' meaning and includes "all aspects of interpretation and commentary as well as appeals to the text's contents in preaching and other forms of persuasive rhetoric" (141). The performative dimension has to do with the performance of scriptures and includes "many ritualized forms of public and private reading, as well as the memorization and recitation of texts" (141). The iconic dimension of scriptures is related to "the physical form, ritual manipulation, and artistic representation of scriptures" (142). Examples of ritualizing scriptures through the iconic dimension include prominent display of scriptures, their processions in palanquins, veneration of them through bowing and kissing, and their manipulation in political ceremonies (142). Watts properly adds that "scriptures have all three dimensions, but different religious groups and individuals ritualize the three dimensions to different degrees" (140).

Watts's model of three dimensions is compact and very effective in showing comprehensively how scriptures are ritualized by religious people. Since he first published this model in 2008, it has helped scholars pay more attention to two important aspects of ritualizing scriptures which had been neglected in academia for a very long time, namely the iconic and performative dimensions. In this book, I accept the terms and categories of Watts's three dimensions for describing Korean cases, but I also try not to force Korean examples into Watts's specific and detailed explanations.

For instance, based on Korean examples, I will correct Watts's argument that oral epics "have no iconic dimension because they are not physical objects" though they are "performed ritually in many cultures" (Watts 2006 [2008], 145) by showing that religious people try to represent oral scriptures by iconic physical objects. Watts also points out that non-textual symbols, such as a cross or a flag, are subject to ritual manipulation and display which correspond to the iconic dimension. These non-textual symbols, according to Watts, do not encode language and so they lack a semantic dimension and have no performative dimension. However, in my observation of Korean cases, things are more complicated than this. As I will explain in Chapter 5 on the Korean shamanic ritual of *seolwi-seolgyeong*, recited oral texts can be embodied as physical objects and can be physically materialized. Shamans practicing in the Chungcheong provinces of Korea make paper figures of main characters in the scriptures, usually powerful gods, write their names and divine positions on paper, and make complicate paper figures representing their weapons as described in scriptures. In the original version of Chapter 5, I wrote that "written texts" are ritualized in *seolwi-seolgyeong* as the title "Performing Scriptures: Ritualizing Written Texts in *Seolwi-seolgyeong*" suggests (Yoo 2019). However, I omitted the word "written" in this book because it occurred to me that shamans of this area have not used the texts in book form for a long time. They received scriptures orally from their teachers, who had also received them orally, and recite them in shamanic rituals. The shamanic scriptures in the Chungcheong provinces of Korea have been ritualized orally without any codex or printed books, though many of the oral scriptures have their origin in Daoist scriptures that have surely been in book form.

This paper figure is remarkable in two respects. First, it is a symbol and at once a real presence (see Yoo 2023, 206–208). Second, it is a non-textual symbol that is based on the contents of scriptures. Religious people who cannot read and write have received and used sacred texts orally for several hundred years. They have developed ways of making the contents of their oral texts into physical objects. By interpreting the semantic dimension of oral texts, they successfully find ways to ritualize them in the iconic dimension. Considering that the figures are necessary for the

Explaining Sacred Texts and Religion by Using Korean Examples

ritual performances of shamans in the area, the performative dimension is based on ritualizing the iconic dimension on the basis of the contents of scriptures, the semantic dimension. The sacred authority of oral scriptures can guarantee the iconic status of physical objects. Some might guess that the contents of the oral texts are made into and represented by physical objects of paper figures due to their original book form. However, this is not a persuasive assumption because we can find examples in other areas of Korea, including the Jeju Province, where the contents of shamanic oral texts that have never had any written form are made into paper figures.

Another of Watts's ideas I would like to extend is his usage of the term "performative" and the category of the performative dimension. About twelve years after he presented the model of three dimensions, Watts showed a suspicion about his own term "performative" and suggested that it should be changed to "expressive." According to Watts, "the word 'performative'... is overly broad and easily confused with ritual performances more generally" and it "also engages a wide range of theoretical considerations" that he did not presuppose. To "focus attention more narrowly on how people express the contents of texts mentally, orally, visually and dramatically," he argued that the phrase "expressive dimension" is more appropriate (Watts 2019, 14 fn18; Watts and Yoo 2021, 1). While I admit that expressive may be more suitable for presenting the way religious people ritualize scriptures as Watts wants to emphasize, I think that "performative," rather than being "overly broad," is still needed to designate a more specific way of ritualizing texts.

As I will show in Chapter 3 in the case of public scripture reading rituals in early Korean Protestantism, scripture is performatively ritualized in J. L. Austin's sense of performative speech. According to Austin, "...to utter the sentence (in, of course, the appropriate circumstances) is not to *describe* my doing of what I should be said in so uttering to be doing or to state that I am doing it: it is to do it" (Austin 1962, 6, emphasis Austin's). The necessary conditions of performative utterances, which are stipulated by Austin, are fulfilled through ritualizing the activity of reading and ritualizing the Bible itself. In the third chapter, I will demonstrate how the Bible readings operate as performative utterances by comparing the Korean scripture reading ritual with some examples of African healing rituals and applying several important ritual theories to the scripture reading ritual. It should be called the performative dimension of scriptures if religious people's utterance of scriptures performs something. Especially in the process of a specific ritual, we can see that recitations or readings of scriptures often create results in the lives of religious people, which may or may not be related to the contents of uttered scriptures. Performing scriptures in ritual context often "causes what it signifies," with or without relation to the semantic understanding of the text. Using Nansy Jay's words, some utterances, including recitations, of scriptures do "not merely express a pre-existing social structural reality in words" but they can call "it into being in deed" (Jay 1992, 6–7, 37). Scriptures are often performatively, not only expressively, ritualized.

Again, Watts's model of the three dimensions of scriptures is a highly useful tool for explaining non-semantic aspects of scriptures and has formed a theoretical basis for reorienting the focus of studying scriptures. Simultaneously, this model should be extended and elaborated through many examples from various religious traditions. Korean examples of ritualization of scriptures will serve for redescribing and rectifying Watts's groundbreaking model.

Affect theory, the materialistic turn, and studying religion

For the last two decades, Watts and other members of SCRIPT have expanded the scope of studying scriptures, from studies focusing only on the semantic aspect to those delving into the iconic and the performative aspects. During the same period, similar endeavors have been made by other theorists of religion who pay more attention to non-linguistic aspects than linguistic ones for understanding and explaining things related to the lives of religious people. Some of these scholars advocate for "affect theory" and emphasize that the affects and animality of human beings are more important to understanding human religious activities than intelligence and other aspects that are related to human consciousness. Donovan O. Schaefer strongly advocates affect theory and tries to explain religion based on it in *Religious Affects: Animality, Evolution, and Power* (2015).

Before I examine Schaefer's perspective, I would like to look at one example of applying affect theory from Schaefer and others to ritualizing the non-semantic dimensions of scriptures. In "How the Bible Feels: The Christian Bible as Effective and Affective Object" (2012 [2017]), Dorina Miller Parmenter relates Protestants' ritualization of the iconic dimension of the Bible to affect theory. Parmenter says,

> For Protestants, the Bible is an indispensable object, for only through the Bible is the promise of salvation available. This affective quality, the feeling that the Bible is an agent of salvation, is cultivated through the iconic dimension of scripture; or, to put it another way, material and visual interactions with the Bible reflect and produce an orientation toward that object as that which promises a good life, that which saves. ...

Explaining Sacred Texts and Religion by Using Korean Examples

> In the example of my student taking her unread Bible to war, it is likely that her action was affect-based or a response to an impulse triggered by past social experiences, **rather than** cognitively-based. The physical form of the Bible protects and comforts, so that she feels safe.
> (Parmenter 2012 [2017], 34–35, emphasis mine)

In the above passage, Parmenter asserts that her former-soldier student's action was affect-based, "rather than cognitive-based." Like many other Protestants who had "the prior affective response and orientation to touching the Bible as good" in their childhood (35), the student felt safe thanks to her material interactions with the Bible, actions that produced an orientation to it that promises a good life.

I agree with her that the affective quality can be produced by past social experiences, through which religious people feel the religious book as good. However, even if it is true that the feeling that the Bible is good is "a response to an impulse triggered by past social experiences," it cannot help being cognitively-based also, at least somewhat, as well as affect-based. To show that the affective quality produced by social experiences is also related to human cognition, I would like to resort to Dan Sperber's explanation of social experiences. Sperber, who is a naturalist and cognitive scientist, says that social experiences are based on "mental representations" and "public representations." While most of mental representations "are found in only one individual," some "get communicated: that is, first transformed by the communicator into public representations, and then re-transformed by the audience into mental representations" (Sperber 1996, 25). If some representations "spread out in a human population, and may end up being instantiated in every member of the population for several generations," they become social-cultural representations (25). In brief, social experiences are formed through a long cognitive process of representing, communicating, and transforming. We cannot exclude the cognition involved in both mental representations and public representations in explaining the affective quality that is produced by past social experiences.

We need to consider many other theories and examples if we would assert that an action is affect-based rather than cognitively-based. The affective quality is inextricably linked to non-affective, linguistic, and cognitive qualities. Therefore, I suggest Parmenter's "rather than" be changed to "along with."

We should also be careful when trying to conclude that one of the dimensions of scriptures may lead independently to certain results. Scriptures, like other religious objects, are recognized as sacred through the comingling of plural aspects in the lives of religious people. In addition, plural dimensions of scripture are apt to work together when a text is ritualized. If the semantic and performative dimensions of a text are ritualized, it often becomes easier for it to be recognized as iconic also by religious people. In this sense, Parmenter is right when she admits that Christians' experiences with the Bible are supposed to be "undoubtedly tied to the semantic and performative dimensions of the text" (Parmenter 2012 [2017], 34). But she implies that affects are related to the iconic dimension of scripture, not others, by saying that "this affective quality, the feeling that the Bible is an agent of salvation, is cultivated through the iconic dimension of scripture." She emphasizes again that "this production of affect is one of the primary functions of the iconic dimension of scripture" (35). However, in order to show how positive social experiences with the Bible are created by the community that accepts its sacred status, we should consider all three dimensions of scriptures functioning together. Affects can be produced not only by touching the Bible, but also by listening to the sound of it being read (which is not possible without being performed) and by learning lessons and getting knowledge from the Bible. Christians of the underground church in North Korea are not able to obtain the Bible in book form. Some members of the church are known to memorize passages or even whole books from the Bible and orally transmit them to other members. Though many Christians of North Korea cannot ritualize the iconic dimension of the Bible, they can have "the feeling that the Bible is an agent of salvation," which Parmenter regards as affective. In the following chapters, therefore, I will pay more attention to how iconic, performative, and semantic aspects of scripture work together than to how those aspects are distinguished from each other.

"Rather than," which is an expression of subtraction, is also repeatedly used by Schaefer in emphasizing affect in religion. Though Schaefer deals with not only religious texts but religion in general, it is necessary to examine his argument to understand how affect theory explains religion and how it can be applied to scripture. He stresses that religion is "not only about language, books, or belief" but "about the way things feel, the things we want... [is] made up of clustered material forms, aspects of our embodied life" (Schaefer 2015, 3). This expression of "not only" does not bother me. However, when he says that religion is "something that puts us in continuity with other animal bodies, **rather than** something that sets us apart" (Schaefer 2015, 3, emphasis mine), he pushes us to choose non-linguistic aspects in religion over linguistic ones. The expression "rather than" may lead us to think that what distinguishes us from animals is not important for studying religion.

Explaining Sacred Texts and Religion by Using Korean Examples

Schaefer begins his book by introducing the primatologist Jane Goodall's observations of the chimpanzees of the Kakombe valley. When the animals saw a magnificent waterfall, according to Goodall, they stopped walking and began to dance, which seemed to her to be a display of "similar feelings of awe that gave rise to the first animistic religions" (Schaefer 2015, 4). Agreeing with Goodall, Schaefer argues that "the location of affect as a determining element of religion... is not confined to chimpanzees." He tries to think about "animality and emotion together" to explore human religion. He asserts that "a turn to affect can help us better understand human religion as animal" (Schaefer 2015, 3).

According to Schaefer, affect is "the flow of forces through bodies outside of, prior to, or underneath language" (4) and "can be understood as the propulsive elements of experience, thought, sensation, feeling, and action that are not necessarily captured or capturable by language or self-sovereign 'consciousness'" (Schaefer 2015, 23). He and his colleagues see affect as "something that is not determined by linguistic effects," (Schaefer 2015, 31) which is critical for understanding religion. While some scholars of affect theory insist that "affect and emotion must be separated," Schaefer traces "affect as something felt" and does not draw "a hard line between affect and emotion" (Schaefer 2015, 26, 32). This emphasis on affect in studying religion would not sound unfamiliar to many students of religion who have read the 18th century classics on the philosophy of religion, such as David Hume's *The Natural History of Religion* (1757) and Friedrich Schleiermacher's *On Religion: Speeches to its Cultured Despisers* (1799) or, later, Rudolf Otto's *The Idea of the Holy* (1917). I think Schaefer and others' suggestion for turning to affect is timely, reasonable, and valuable because theories of religion in the twentieth century relied so heavily on linguistic ideas and terms while relatively neglecting feeling and intuition. This tendency is clearly seen even in Jonathan Z. Smith's argument that understanding of religion should be based on expression and representation (Smith 2004, 102–103, 363).

However, when Schaefer regards linguistic and intellectual elements as subservient to affective ones, he resonates with scholars of former generations who were full of confidence in defining the essence of religion. He and other affect theorists obviously refuse to see what sets human beings apart from other animals while stressing the continuity. Affect theory highlights the importance of "the world without the application of language" (Schaefer 2015, 15), which leads to the exclusion of language and consciousness without presenting persuasive grounds. Schaefer boldly argues about the sources of morality by stating that "prior to language, moral decision making—in human and other animals—is produced from embodied regimes of affect" (Schaefer 2015, 133), but this assertion is based on circular reasoning whose hypothesis is presented as its conclusion. Based on affect theory that articulates the world without the application of language, the cause of morality is concluded as arising prior to language.

It is true that Schaefer presses an important point that has been overlooked in the field of studying religion. Scholars of SCRIPT also have articulated that focusing on the semantic dimension is not enough for studying scriptures and have emphasized non-linguistic qualities of ritualizing scriptures. However, for a comprehensive understanding of religion and specifically of scriptures, the discontinuity of humans with other animals should be paid attention to along with the continuity. Though Schaefer sometimes uses phrases like "affects as well as language" (Schaefer 2015, 12), in effect he is talking about affects "rather than" language. He urges us to attend to "the world *without* the application of language" by advocating that "affect theory suggests that our animal intimacy with the world *precedes* constitution inside a linguistic frame" (15, emphasis mine). To him, affect always has priority in terms of the time sequence of its appearance as well as its importance. Moral decision making is produced by affect "*prior to* language" (Schaefer 2015, 133, emphasis mine). Again, it is very important to pay attention to animality and materiality, which have not been considered enough in studying religion. However, even when we try to illuminate human animality based on theories of evolution, we should not disregard how linguistic and intellectual qualities work together with affect.

In academia, especially in the humanities, religion has commonly been regarded as what human beings seek, do, and think about. Therefore, ways of understanding religion have been bound up with ways of understanding human beings. Along with the continuity of humans with other animals in religion, which affect theory emphasizes by arguing the priority of affect over language, we should take note of differences between humans and other animals, something also very clearly seen in religion. Yuval Noah Harari goes further and stresses the differences between our own species, *Homo sapiens*, and other human species, such as Neanderthals and Denisovans, "in their cognitive and social abilities" (Harari 2015, 18-19) based on which he demonstrates what religion did for prehistoric people. Harari asserts that "*Homo sapiens* conquered this world thanks above all to its unique language (Schaefer 2015, 21)." He agrees with many researchers who believe that Sapiens' unprecedented accomplishments were "the

Explaining Sacred Texts and Religion by Using Korean Examples

product of a revolution in Sapiens' cognitive abilities" (Schaefer 2015, 23). Sapiens came to have "a new type of language" that made them gossip much more effectively than other human species and have "more sophisticated types of cooperation" (Schaefer 2015, 26). He emphasizes "the truly unique feature of our language" which enables Sapiens "to transmit information about things that do not exist at all." This linguistic ability distinguished Sapiens from the others, enabling them to talk about "entire kinds of entities that they have never seen, touched or smelled" (Schaefer 2015, 27). According to Harari, this ability brought religious beliefs and myths into being. It was thanks to myths that Sapiens could obtain "the unprecedented ability to cooperate flexibly in large numbers" (Schaefer 2015, 27), and it was religion that has granted "super human legitimacy" to otherwise fragile social structures (Schaefer 2015, 234). Just as Harari shows, linguistic and cognitive qualities, by which human beings collectively have imagined myths, may be as important as affect in understanding religion. To understand and explain religion, not only should continuity between humans and other animals be considered, but differences as well.

Affect theory is closely related to "the materialist shift in religious studies" (Schaefer 2015, 4). Manuel A. Vásquez's perspective, as seen in his major book *More than Belief: A Materialist Theory of Religion* (2011), accords with the theoretical standpoint of the affect theory in that he also stresses the non-linguistic aspects of the world or, more specifically, the religious world. According to Vásquez, the world "is *not just language... rather*, what we understand the world to be like is determined by many things," among which he includes our sensory organs, our ability to manipulate objects, and our interactions with our environment (Vásquez 2011, 11, 14, emphasis mine).

However, Vásquez actually does not show "what we understand the world to be like is determined by many things" in his book. The main purpose of "the materialist turn" advocated by Vásquez is the "rematerialization of the study of religion" (Vásquez 2011, 87). He argues that religious studies should be conducted within a materialist framework "rather than simply approaching religion as private belief" (Vásquez 2011, 3). In order to work towards this goal, Vásquez devotes the whole book to explaining his non-reductive materialist epistemological framework and to comparing other philosophical perspectives on the materialist view. He says that theories should be put forward "for a more therapeutic purpose," by which he means "to disentangle some of the epistemological knots that have characterized the discipline of religion" (Vásquez 2011, 9). While emphasizing the importance of the materialist perspective, in practice he mainly deals with various philosophical approaches related to materialism. I will introduce what Vásquez pursues in his book by using his own words: highlighting "key ideas, arguments, and methods at stake in order to frame current approaches to the body" (Vásquez 2011, 21); showing "how transcendental subjectivism and foundational idealism in phenomenology as a philosophical movement reinforced anti-materialist and anti-somatic tendencies within the phenomenology or religion and history of religion" (Vásquez 2011, 87); exploring "some important versions of social constructionism in an effort to build an approach that... does not fall into a self-defeating reductionism" (Vásquez 2011, 124); tracing "the evolution of social constructionism" (Vásquez 2011, 149), focusing "on the epistemologies at stake and on the implications they have for a non-reductive materialist framework in the study of religion" (Vásquez 2011, 174); criticizing "Geertz's approach to religion" and showing that he "gave rise to a strong version of 'textualism'" (Vásquez 2011, 213); articulating the "modern understanding of praxis," especially that of Karl Marx who emphasized its dynamic nature (Vásquez 2011, 232). In brief, his materialism does not directly show or even mention "many things," like our sensory organs or our interactions in our environment, but instead focuses on theoretical critiques.

Vásquez's strongest criticism is addressed to scholars of the previous generation, such as Mircea Eliade and Ninian Smart, whom he calls "phenomenologists of religion," for emphasizing "values and beliefs" that they argued "constitute the core of religion" (Vásquez 2011, 106) and for not laying stress on human bodies, senses, and concrete objects. According to Vásquez, these phenomenologists are responsible for "the somatophobic internalism and idealism that has dominated much of the contemporary study of religion" (Vásquez 2011, 105). "This internalism and idealism" persistently puts emphasis "on religious meaning and worldviews."

However, Vásquez should be criticized in the same way he attacks Eliade and Smart that values and beliefs in religion come to be neglected by giving too much prominence to materialism. A turn from a theoretical position emphasizing one dimension to the opposite position is liable to end up disregarding the former. Joanne Punzo Waghorne calls this sort of conflict between two opposite academic perspectives a "civil war." According to Waghorne, "we [scholars of religious studies] are at war with ourselves and within ourselves. The signs of that draining civil war are everywhere" (Waghorne 2004, 77). To end this civil war, we must consider and admit that dimensions of religion, on which the criticizing scholar himself or herself does not focus, may play important roles in the lives of religious people. Not only the feelings, senses, and concrete objects, but the values and beliefs of religious people should also be considered to properly understand the ritualization of religious texts. Rather than the assertion of "rather than," different qualities or dimensions of religion should be put together.

In a recently published article, I argued that we should avoid the expression "not... but" because, although it sounds persuasive, it is often inexact. I suggested that Robert Orsi's idea of a real presence, which he strictly distinguishes from a symbol, should be rectified because a symbol can also be experienced as a real presence in the lives of religious people (Yoo 2023, 206–208). Orsi criticizes theories of religion in which "the gods really present ... with whom humans have been in relationship in different times and places" have been explained as "symbols, signs, metaphors, functions, and abstractions" (Orsi 2016, 4). He objects to reducing the sacred beings in the experience of religious people to symbols or signs. However, his strict separation between the real and the symbolic should be reconsidered. Orsi knows that "the divide ... between the real and the symbolic" also "defines the modern temperament" (Orsi 2016, 37). But he himself adheres to the modern, narrow meaning of the symbol. Though he says, "the symbol is not an experience of something, but a sign or a representation of it" (38), for many religious people, representing can be an important way of experiencing. I demonstrated this by expounding the divine and material characteristics of *mengdu*, the main set of ritual instruments of the *simbang* (shaman of Jeju, Korea). To summarize, *mengdu* are a set of brass instruments yet at the same time something else, as is characteristic of symbols. Jeju people know that *mengdu* are a physical item and yet they also believe it to be something extraordinary. *Mengdu* are believed to hold the power of a deity and even to be an independent deity enshrined in the *simbang*'s house to whom offering are made. Though Orsi suggests the notion of a real presence that is not a symbol, sacred objects are often a symbol and simultaneously a real presence itself.

As will be seen in the next chapter, in the "Gagugyeonghaeng (or Gyeonghaeng)" ritual, which can be translated into English as "the parade of sutra," a copy of the *Benign King Prajna Sutra* was placed in a huge, splendidly decorated palanquin just as if it was the Buddha himself. Though people participating in the parade knew that the copy was not literally the Buddha, they believed it to be a replacement for the Buddha and that it held the power of the Buddha. As such, it was revered as the Buddha himself. Chapters of this volume describe many examples in which religious people ritualize sacred books in multiple ways, regarding them as sacred beings and simultaneously as symbols of sacred beings.

For pursuing a comprehensive understanding of scriptures, we should be careful not to employ the expression "not... but" or "rather than" so easily. A turn of focus from one dimension that most scholars have concentrated on to other dimensions that have been neglected by most scholars should be welcome as it helps us expand the range of our vision. It should not, however, lead us to disregard the importance of the old focus. Undue criticism of scholars who paid attention to values, beliefs, and aspirations may lead to a failure to see how religious people relate bodies and objects to internal ideas. Scriptures are experienced and ritualized not in one single way because they include various aspects. They are concrete objects in most cases, they contain beliefs and values, and they are simultaneously experienced through human senses and cognition. Emphasizing any one aspect should not lead to ignoring others.

Towards a comprehensive theory of sacred texts

Religious people create, develop, read, recite, think about, study, feel, revere, and appropriate their sacred texts. Therefore, we must consider the many qualities related to each moment in human lives, including intellectual, linguistic, sensual, and affective, to understand and explain how scriptures are ritualized by religious people.

Though the change of subject may seem abrupt, I would like to recount a story about a cat named Wallace, which I heard from my old teacher. It is a story about the reactions of an animal to a specific situation, which seem to be similar to reactions that are encountered in human religious experiences. Long before affect theory began to influence religious studies, students in the Department of Religious Studies at Seoul National University had the chance to think about the continuity between human beings and other animals. The late Professor Yiheum Yun, who taught at SNU from 1980 to 2005, liked to ask students if human religious experience is limited to only humans. As is well known, Rudolf Otto argued that numinous experience, whose object religious people feel as wholly other, involves both fear and fascination. From the early 1980s, Yun asserted that animals can also have this fear and fascination when they meet some trembling objects, just as Schaefer tried to show by quoting Jane Goodall's assessment of the chimpanzee waterfall dance. Yun used his own observation to support his argument. While he was a graduate student in the USA, one of his neighbors raised a cat named Wallace that had lived with him in his apartment. When the neighbor had to visit his family far away, he asked Yun to care for Wallace. Yun took Wallace out to a lakeside park and was surprised to see how Wallace reacted to a totally new situation. Going outside of the

Explaining Sacred Texts and Religion by Using Korean Examples

home for the first time, according to Yun's observation, Wallace was all in a dither, hesitating to come out of the crate. Yun said that he must have felt both fear and fascination, which did not look different from the so-called ontological shock that human religious experience is said to involve.

Based on this instance and other observation of animals, Yun emphasized the importance of animality and affect in religious experience from the early 1980s. Some students agreed with Yun's argument while others did not. But most students admitted that Yun's argument was persuasive. When he talked about animality and affect in religious experience, Yun always pointed out that religious experience cannot be regarded as religion itself, though it is an important element of religion. Yun said religions are like a tripod and must contain three elements. I will not introduce his "tripodal" theory of religion here, which I myself do not think is a very effective tool for explaining religion. What I want to underline is that his advice not to explain religion by magnifying just one of multiple elements was very helpful for me in studying religion. To explain religion comprehensively and properly, we should consider non-linguistic aspects, such as affects and emotions. But highlighting affective qualities should not lead us to disregard other elements or count them as secondary. Emphasizing only rational aspects or only irrational aspects of religion would not be a balanced approach to the study of religion, which is a very complex and multi-layered conglomeration of various elements.

I appreciate recent works of scholars who propose "the new subfield of material religion," which should not be "confused with the materialist shift" of Vásquez (Schaefer 2015, 111). These scholars have made a significant contribution to the field of religious studies by taking notice of the importance of concrete objects in religion. They properly underscore "a dynamic interplay between language, sensing bodies, and things in the world" (Schaefer 2015, 112). I also think highly of the importance of this dynamic interplay. However, when they try to "put materiality at the forefront of the understanding of religion" (Meyer, Morgan, Paine, and Plate 2011, 6), they in effect treat other aspects of religion as secondary or minor. For instance, S. Brent Plate defines religion as "deriving from rudimentary human experiences, from lived, embodied practices," which then can be modified and retouched by language (Plate 2014, 15). He is assigning precedence or priority to non-linguistic qualities, just as affect theorists do. While dynamic displays between language and things are vividly observable phenomena, a precedence of things over language is at best a plausible hypothesis. For a scholar to show precedence and priority to certain elements found in religion, elaborated theories and strong evidence should be provided. Dynamic interplays between language and material objects should be paid attention to and explained because they are plainly shown in what religious people adopt, regard, and appropriate, especially in religious texts.

Religious texts are certainly composed of language, and still they encompass various non-linguistic aspects, but the linguistic and the non-linguistic elements are inseparably bound together in them. Religious texts provide arenas in which linguistic qualities work together with material, sensual, affective, and emotional qualities to create scenes for religious people. Studies on the iconic and the performative dimensions of scripture can vividly demonstrate how these different qualities are comingled to be ritualized. Cases from Korean religious texts in this book will show how linguistic aspects are related to non-linguistic ones. For instance, intellectuals are inclined to stress the contents, but they also often mobilize non-linguistic qualities to help ritualize these contents. As I will delve into in Chapter 4, Confucian scholars during the Joseon Dynasty tried to make the best of their senses for the ideal study and for the full enjoyment of scriptures. It will be shown that they tried to feel the contents, utilizing non-linguistic senses on the basis of the linguistic, semantic dimension. In religious texts, linguistic aspects and non-linguistic aspects are interdependent on each other. In Chapter 5, I will demonstrate that shamans who know the contents of scriptures make paper traps to capture evil spirits as well as paper figures of gods to overpower those spirits, while lay people just look forward to seeing the results from the power of scriptures without knowing the contents.

Furthermore, it will also be attested that religious people have devised some ways of utilizing the power of scriptures which are not related to their contents. As will be described in chapters 2 and 6, just by possessing any form of a scripture, whether it be one-page piece of scripture, a tiny miniature, or splendidly decorated one, many Korean Buddhists believe that they will receive the blessing and power of the Buddha. In this case, the circuit of power exerted by a scripture is often dictated by its iconic status, as well as by the context in which the scripture is ritualized. As will be seen in Chapter 3 which focuses on the public scripture reading ritual in the early Korean Protestantism, a reading of the scripture, which was originally designed for the study of its contents, can be ritualized so that the reading yields results that are not directly related to the contents. On the other hand, we can find cases where the semantic dimension of the text extends its influence on the non-intellectual public for the efficient ritualization of the text. As will be shown in Chapter 7, elite members of the early Donghak could contemplate the contents of the incantation without difficulty while reciting it, even though it was written in classical Chinese. The general public, however, was expected to recite it without knowing the detailed meaning. As the recitation became the central ritual of Donghak for serving God and self-cultivation, the public also ritualized the text both by reciting it and by learning its meaning and interpretation. Cases found in Korean religions will provide good examples showing various ways in which religious texts comingle affect, sensation, and cognition.

Sacred texts in the real lives of religious people in Korea

A theory that explains the lives of religious people should begin with data. Jonathan Z. Smith distinguished four moments in the comparative study of religions among which description is the first. Description is "a double contextualization." In this double process, comparative scholars first locate a given example within its social, historical, and cultural environments. In other words, they first examine and contextualize data. Then they take account of "how scholars have accepted the datum as significant for the purpose of argument" (Smith 2000, 239; 2004, 29). After that, scholars can move on to the description of a second example. Comparison becomes possible with two or more exempla in view. Such a comparison aims at the redescription of the exempla and a rectification of academic categories. The comparative study of religion begins by limiting our focus to a specific aspect of the data to identify a characteristic that should be explored, not by examining religious data through the lens of any assumptions that we may be tempted to use as the starting point for our research (see Smith 1990, 53), Like most presentations and papers produced by members of SCRIPT, each chapter of this volume begins from concrete data which provides grounds for showing the iconic status and the sacred power of scriptures in the lives of religious people. Articulating and contextualizing specific exempla, each of which corresponds to a specific aspect of sacred texts in Korean religions, will lead to the redescription of the exempla and rectifications of categories in use in academia. Each chapter will show how scriptures are ritualized by mixing ways of appropriating them as material objects with values and beliefs, which are often derived from the contents of the scriptures themselves. I expect the following chapters to be helpful for redescribing examples and rectifying categories used by scholars of scriptures in religious studies.

The rest of this volume consists of six examples taken from five Korean religions; two cases from Buddhism and one case each from Protestant Christianity, Confucianism, shamanism, and Donghak. Chapter 2 demonstrates the need to give more attention to the iconic status and the sacred power of Buddhist scripture by describing how lay Korean Buddhists try to appropriate the power of sutras. The oral and aural aspects of scripture, explained by Wilfred Cantwell Smith, provide only a limited understanding of the characteristics of scripture. It should be noted that most lay people before modern times, not only in Buddhist cultures but also in Christian and other traditions, neither had the chance to recite scriptures nor to listen to their recitations regularly. Several clear examples show contemporary Korean Buddhists' acceptance of the iconic status of sutras and their attempt to appropriate the power and status of those sacred texts. In contemporary Korea, this is done by lay Buddhists in daily life by repeating the texts and possessing physical copies of them. Twenty-first-century lay believers who cannot read or recite in the traditional style have found new methods of repetition, such as internet programs for copying sacred texts and for playing recordings of their recitations. In addition, many Korean Buddhists consider the act of having sutras in one's possession to be an effective way of accessing the sacred status and power of these texts. Hence various ways of possessing them have been developed in a wide range of commercial products, from fancy gilded sutras to sneakers embroidered with mantras.

Chapter 3 ferrets out the social function and meaning of performative utterance as illustrated by the Bible study meeting in early twentieth-century Korean Protestantism. The main activity consisted of reading the Bible aloud. Many scholars of the history of Korean Protestantism assert that the Bible study meeting played a crucial role in the rapid growth of Korean Protestantism in the late nineteenth and early twentieth centuries. Most agree that the Bible study meeting promoted "the Great Revival," which led to a fourfold increase in church membership in Korea between the years 1903 and 1907. These meetings have not been widely studied by academics until now. Analysis of Korean public scripture readings from a comparative perspective not only provides a vivid illustration of the social function of the performative dimension of scriptures, but it also suggests the need to further define the meaning of "performative." As to the first point, the particular ways in which the Bible was read in the Korean context contributed to the growing number of converts to Christianity. Bible readings in the context of study groups in early Korean Protestantism facilitated the absorption of Christianity into Korean culture by building on traditional religious practices and by offering a way for native Koreans to take a leadership role in the growth of the new religion. Second, these scripture readings were performative in the way defined by J. L. Austin's theory of

Explaining Sacred Texts and Religion by Using Korean Examples

performative speech and elaborated by Roy Rappaport's description of the indexical function of ritual, because they led to Koreans' conversions to Christianity and strengthened their Christian faith. The necessary conditions for performative utterances, as defined by Austin, were satisfied by ritualizing the activity of reading the Bible itself.

Chapter 4 focuses on sensory readings by Neo-Confucian scholars. Chu Hsi (1130-1200) of China and Yi Hwang (1501-1570) of Korea, leading scholars of the Neo-Confucian schools of each respective country, emphasized readings of Confucian scriptures. They believed that Confucian scriptures have transformative power when read repeatedly and deliberately. Chu introduced the concept—further developed by Yi—of encouraging a scholar to activate at least three senses when reading a text, and promoted it above the experience of merely reading the characters of the text. They advised Neo-Confucian scholars to try to make contact with the sages and fully internalize their teaching through the senses of sight, hearing, and taste when reading scriptures, though they did not directly appeal to the physical senses. First, the text should be recited aloud so that the reciters will hear their own voices, and sometimes those of their colleagues when several scholars read together. They imagined, furthermore, that the voices they were hearing while reading were those of the ancient sages themselves. Secondly, while hearing the voices of the sages, the reciting scholars should visualize their images, seeking personal communion with them. Finally, the meditative reading of scholars was frequently likened to savoring a text's flavor. The act of reading a book was described as eating, biting, chewing, and tasting. When the readers recited the text aloud, pronouncing each syllable using tongues, lips and mouths, they were engaged in a gustatory experience: "chewing" and "tasting" scriptures.

In Chapter 5, a specific ritual named *seolwi-seolgyeong* is investigated. *Seolwi-seolgyeong* is a Korean shamanic ritual in which shamans recite scriptures while seated. This ritual illustrates a comprehensive way of performing scriptures: texts are recited, written, and materialized so that their sacred status is secured and their power is maximized. The recitation is the nucleus of this ritual. Though lay participants do not understand the meaning of the recited scriptures, they regard the recitation as effective because the gods and malevolent spirits are thought to understand it. For *seolwi-seolgyeong* to be most efficacious, the recitation of scriptures should be supported by the materialization of scriptures. Evil spirits become frightened by reading the paper banners on which the names of gods and other words derived from scriptures are written. Geometric paper figures depicting gods visually scare evil spirits and those that reflect the

Korean Religious Texts in Iconic and Performative Rituals

scriptures' cosmology can hedge them in and trap them. In this ritual process, scriptures are privileged and distinguished as sacred beings in several ways. First, scriptures are ritualized when shamans and other participants in *seolwi-seolgyeong* treat the scriptures as no less than the words of the gods. Second, reciting the scripture is equated with the proclamation of divine words. This ritualization is considered more effective when scriptures are recited more skillfully. Third, the contents of scriptures are also ritualized when the contents are considered so sacred as to subdue evil spirits and to heal patients and when shamans materialize the contents into paper figures on the basis of their interpretation of the cosmology and theology in scriptures.

In Chapter 6, I will demonstrate that miniature sutras allow Korean Buddhists to feel the Buddha's presence and protection in their daily lives. Miniature sutras are so small that they are difficult, if not impossible, to read, but these texts are not intended for study. Instead, the mere presence of these miniature sutras is thought to be efficacious. Many Korean Buddhists possess small Buddha statues at home into whose hollow bellies they insert miniature sutras. To those Buddhists, sutras, which are the dharma of the Buddha, activate the statues and turn them into the Buddha himself. In addition, they believe that miniature sutras in their hands or pockets bless them and protect them from evil. Scriptures as the word-body of the Buddha are thought to work for Buddhists irrespective of their semantic content, and without any explicit ritual recitation or repetition.

Chapter 7 deals with the recitation of scripture, usually part of it but sometimes all of it, in Donghak. Most readers of this book will be familiar with the other religions I discuss, but not with Donghak. As I will explain in more detail, Donghak is the name of a religion founded in the late nineteenth century that quickly became widespread in central and southern parts of Korea. I will show that the theology and practices of Donghak were indivisibly intermingled with each other in the recitation of its two basic scriptures, *Donggyeongdaejeon* and *Yongdamyusa*. In the early stage of Donghak, recitation was the most important way of ritually serving God while teaching and publicizing the main myths and doctrines of the sect. It was also the most important means for early members to practice self-cultivation. All early members of Donghak were supposed to recite the incantation (*jumun*) consisting of twenty-one Chinese characters, just as the contemporary adherents of modern denominations derived from Donghak still do. This incantation is included and explained in *Dongyeongdaejeon* and is believed to summarize the core doctrines of Donghak. Reciting this incantation was a way of affirming Donghak members' identification with

Explaining Sacred Texts and Religion by Using Korean Examples

the sect. Members also believed that their recitation was a way of reifying the core doctrine of "Sicheonju," or serving God. The book of *Yongdamyusa* comprises nine pieces of *gasa*, a traditional Korean poetic genre which was meant to be recited aloud. The founder of Donghak, Choe Jeu, composed the *Yongdamyusa* in Korean in order to propagate the doctrines to the public who did not know classical Chinese. *Yongdamyusa* passages were regularly recited by members along with simple tunes and cadences.

I believe that the following chapters provide illuminating examples of ways for ritualizing religious texts. I expect these examples from Korean religions and my theoretical reflections to contribute more small dots to the pointillist painting of scriptures in religious studies, as described by Wendy Doniger (Doniger 2000, 70–72). To obviate "the sorts of problems that arise when we argue from the top down and posit a transcendental agent as the source of cross-cultural congruences," and to avoid universalism that "falsely universalizes an ideological fiction based on the interests of the privileged," Doniger suggests "a pointillism formed from the individual points of individual authors." By this pointillism, according to Doniger, "we can anchor our cross-cultural paradigms in an investigation of the unique insights of particular tellings of our cross-cultural themes." I would like to nuance this passage for this book: the cross-cultural theme of iconic and performative ritualization of scriptures can be anchored in investigations of specific insights garnered by the particular ways that religious people in Korea have devised and appropriated scriptures.

Doniger argued that if we pay attention to the real lives of religious people, "arguing from the bottom up," we can find "more widely shared human bonds and assumptions that transcend ... cultural barriers" (Doniger 1999, 4). Of course, I am aware that dots alone cannot become a picture. To paint a picture using pointillism, painters making dots should share a perspective to produce a rough sketch of the picture. James W. Watts and other colleagues in SCRIPT have developed a rough sketch on the basis of a shared perspective. Beginning from the appreciation of the importance of multi-dimensional approaches to scriptures, we have worked together to conduct cross-cultural comparison and to select "the sorts of questions that might transcend any particular culture" (Doniger 1998, 40). These questions that transcend any particular culture will be answered by scholars marking small dots about specific religious texts of a specific religious community at a specific time. This book demonstrates how these questions about iconic and performative texts can be answered in particular religious communities of Korea. These numerous dots will lead us to see similarities between ritual usages of scriptures in various cultures, or "construct a continuum" of them, and also to articulate differences (Doniger, 1998, 35). Examples from Korean religions in this volume clarify scriptures' iconic and performative dimensions that are ritualized in correlation with the semantic dimension, a correlation that can be seen in the continuum of many cultures, and also accentuate the characteristic and distinctive colors of Korean religions.

2

POSSESSION AND REPETITION: HOW KOREAN LAY BUDDHISTS APPROPRIATE SCRIPTURES

The iconic status and power of sutras in Buddhism

Just like scriptures of many other religions, a Buddhist sutra is itself a sacred object rather than just a written book. Buddhist scriptures enjoy a status equivalent to that of the Buddha as his representation. This is a well known fact among Koreans and people from other cultures in which Buddhism constitutes an essential part. Korean high school students learn in national history class that in the eleventh century, the Goryeo Dynasty (918-1392) commissioned engraving of the *Tripitaka* on wooden blocks and printed it in order to obtain Buddha's protection against the Mongolian invasion, rather than to study or teach the contents of the scripture. Moreover, Koreans who have interests in cultural heritage know about the tradition of putting Buddhist sutras into the stupas of Korean temples. A stupa, originally a burial place for relics of the Buddha, has been equated with his body and revered as an object of worship. Sutras can replace the relics in stupas because many Buddhists identify the Buddha with his teaching, dharma, and believe that the book of his teaching is no different from his body.

The iconic status and power of written texts that represent the Buddha himself have been acknowledged by Korean Buddhists for a long time. This is manifest in the "Gagugyeonghaeng (or Gyeonghaeng)" ritual, which can be translated into English as "the parade of sutra." It began in 1046 and continued until the following dynasty, Joseon, started to repress Buddhism. According to *The History of the Goryeo Dynasty*, the Goryeo court performed this ritual in the second month of the lunar calendar for the purpose of driving away disasters and diseases from the capital city Gaeseong. The main part of this ritual was the parade of Buddhist monks, government ministers, high officials, and many citizens marching around the capital. It was headed by a splendidly decorated huge palanquin in which a copy of *Benign King Prajna Sutra* was placed just as if it was the Buddha himself. Monks recited the sutra when they paraded through the city. It is recorded that in 1106, a long spell of dry weather came to an end when many citizens of the capital performed Gyeonghaeng. The king was pleased and praised the power of this ritual (Choi 1996, 29; "Gagugyeonghaeng" 1983, 37).

This example demonstrates that the people of Goryeo considered the sutra as the embodiment of the Buddha and that people recognized and attempted to appropriate its power. Though people of the time knew that the sutra was not the Buddha himself, they accepted it as a replacement of the Buddha. In that sense, the sutra was the real presence and at once the symbol of the Buddha. According to Louis Dupré, symbols represent the signified object "in the double sense of making present and taking the place of" (Dupré 2000, 1). Sacred objects such as a copy of *the Benign King Prajna Sutra*, as symbols of the sacred, make it possible for religious people to experience the sacred, as Clifford Geertz said, "by formulating conceptions of a general order of existence and clothing those conceptions with such an aura of factuality that the moods and motivations seem uniquely realistic" (Geertz 1973, 90). A sacred text remains itself as a book and simultaneously is accepted as something else.

Despite the widely acknowledged iconic status and magical power of sutras in the history of Buddhism, most scholars of Buddhism and historians of religions have neglected these important aspects of sutras. An examination of six textbooks that are used for introduction courses to Buddhism at American college and university reveals that none explain the status, function, or power of Buddhist scriptures. All six books deal mainly with the contents of scriptures and their process of canonization (Gethin 1998, 35–58; Mitchell 2002, 64–94; Harvey 1990, 73–120; Robinson and Johnson 1997, 51–55; Williams 2000, 1–40; Strong 2002, 88–175). Korean scholars of religion have also largely overlooked the function, status, and power of Buddhist scripture.

It is true that some scholars have shown an interest in how the Buddhist scriptures were accepted and appropriated by early Indian Mahayana Buddhists. Instead of studying the doctrines, teachings, or philosophy contained in sutras, they have focused on the ritual context in which sutras came to acquire the status of the Buddha and magical power (Schopen 1991, 1–22).[1] In *Beyond the Written Word*, William Graham mentions the "cult of the book that may once have existed in India alongside or even in com-

---

1. Schopen points out that Western scholars have mainly relied on literary material and disregarded a large body of archaeological and epigraphical material because they have been influenced by the Protestant assumption which values the contents of textual sources.

petition with the more familiar relic cult in early Mahayana tradition" (Graham 1987, 61). Though he cites some studies on Japanese and Tibetan Buddhism, he does not point out that the so called "cult of the book" can be found in almost every Buddhist culture, including that of Korea. Richard Gombrich argues that the rise of Mahayana was due to the emergence of written tradition and that the early Mahayana texts were able to survive because they were written down. The beginning of Mahayana, one of the most significant events in the history of Buddhism, was caused by a change in the way of keeping sutras rather than by controversies over doctrines (Gombrich 1990). Further developing Gombrich's argument, Will Tuladhar-Douglas claims that "the ritual conundrum of written texts was constitutive of Mahayana Buddhism" and that Mahayana sutras were reproduced because each book was recognized as a deity (Tuladhar-Douglas 2009, 250). Contemporary examples should be added to the historical ones that Schopen, Gombrich and Tuladhar-Douglas call attention to. In addition, theoretical explanations need to be developed for Buddhists' appropriation of the iconic status and sacred power of sutras.

This essay examines the ways in which Korean Buddhists attempt to appropriate the power of sutras in order to demonstrate the importance of the iconic status and function of scriptures for contemporary Buddhists. The abundant examples available from Korean Buddhism will also help us suggest a theoretical explanation for this phenomenon. First, I will point out that while Wilfred Cantwell Smith and his followers, including William Graham, have rightly recognized the importance of the function and status of scriptures, they limited their analysis of the topic for the most part to the oral and aural aspects of scriptures. It should be noted that most lay persons before modern times, not only in Buddhist cultures but also in Christendom and other places, did not have many chances to recite scriptures or even to hear recitations regularly. The oral and aural repetitions of sacred books were privileges enjoyed only by religious elites, mainly priests and monks, though the common people devised their own methods of repetition, such as by reciting abbreviated versions of sutras, such as *dharani* and mantra.[2]

---

2. *Dharani*, which is translated into Korean as *Neungji* or *Chongji*, indicates a passage that summarizes the basic principles of a long sutra. *Dharani* is believed to have been originally made in order to help people remember the teaching of a sutra. The recitation of *dharani* creates the same meritorious effect as reading the entire original version. Thus *dharani* passages cannot be understood separately from the text of scriptures. In a broad sense, *dharani* includes mantra, which is translated into Korean as "*Jineon.*" In general, shorter passages (or even words or syllables) are called mantra and longer ones *dharani*. More strictly speaking though, mantra means Sanskrit passages or words that are phonetically read and used like a spell. Buddhists believe the recita-

Next, I will provide several examples of contemporary Korean Buddhists' appreciation of the iconic aspect of sutras and appropriation of their power and status. Contemporary Korean Buddhists have developed various ways of possessing scriptures in which neither reading nor reciting plays an essential role. On the basis of these examples, I will argue that repetition and possession have been two important ways in which people appropriate the sacred power of scriptures. Korean Buddhism in the twenty-first century provides lay persons who cannot read or recite sutras with new means for copying sacred texts and listening to recitations, often by means of the internet. It will also be shown that possessing sutras is considered an effective way of taking its power and sacred status for oneself.

The theoretical problem of scriptures for those who cannot read or recite

In 1971, Wilfred Cantwell Smith pointed out that scholars of the Bible in liberal-arts departments of religion should consider the Bible as scripture and scripture itself as a generic phenomenon. Smith argued that they should treat scripture "as a religious form" and "a living force in the life of the Church." According to Smith, scholars should study the cultural significance of scripture and the roles that it plays in the life of religious people. We should also find out what gives scripture sacred status and what people do with the Bible now (Smith 1971). Smith is right. Adherents of religions do not limit their use of scripture to interpreting its contents alone. They accept their scripture as a sacred being or a representation of it, and attempt to utilize its power. As Smith has stated, it is the task of a scholar of comparative religion to suggest general explanations for the significance, status, roles and functions of scripture in the life of religious people. The question that I address in this essay is a more specific version of Smith's question: What do Korean Buddhists who cannot read their scripture do in order to experience its power? I will describe various ways of appropriating sutras which have been developed for, or even by, Korean lay Buddhists who are not able to read the written text.

In another work, Smith criticized Western scholarship for neglecting the various forms, concepts, and roles of scripture. He also asserted that scripture should not only be understood as "a written sacred book" but should also be examined in the context of "oral/aural tradition" (Smith 1989, 30, 35-36). However, the focus of Smith and other scholars who agree with his assertion on oral/aural tradition cannot provide explanations for all the

---

tion of mantra itself produces an effect even if the person reciting does not know the meaning of passage.

different roles that scriptures play in the religious life of believers and all the meanings accorded to these sacred texts.

In *Rethinking Scripture: Essays from a Comparative Perspective*, a group of scholars who had been influenced by Smith carried out an in-depth study on the significance and role of scripture as their mentor had suggested (Levering 1989). The contributors tried to apply Smith's comparative perspective to their research field. Graham, in a chapter of this book and his book *Beyond Written Words*, asserts that we must pay attention to scripture's function as text "in the oral and aural round of daily life" (Graham 1987, 156; Graham 1989). He also says, "the most important result of attention to the oral dimension of scripture is to make more vivid the intensely personal engagement of a community with its sacred text" (Graham 1987, 162). But the oral and aural dimensions of scripture cannot give a satisfactory answer to his own question "how do we discern the ways in which scripture has penetrated into those sectors or religious life that lie outside the more or less elitist domains of the literati or intellectuals" (Graham 1987, 163). It is obvious that the oral/aural aspect of scripture should necessarily be considered in order to understand forms and roles of religious scripture. However, as I mentioned above, in many traditional religious communities, members who could recite scripture or read it out loud had been few in number. The number of people who could listen to the recitation of scripture regularly was also quite limited. The situation for some contemporary communities has not changed much. Therefore, if we pay attention to only oral/aural aspect of scripture, we still miss many of the ways that lay believers' view and use of scripture.

I do not intend to diminish the importance of Graham's contribution to the study of religious text. Graham properly attempts to explain religious scriptures in relationship to "men and women of faith." He indicates that no text can be called "scripture" in and of itself and that a religious text acquires its ultimate and transcendent status, namely "scripturality," through interactions with religious people (Graham 1987, 5–6). I also think that his focus on the function of the oral dimension of the written scriptural text is important. By emphasizing this dimension, he successfully overcomes academia's conventional inclination toward studying the literary content of religious texts. He expects "the strong orality of scriptures" to reveal "the functional meaning of scriptural texts in religious life" and argues that this functional meaning is tied to "folk appropriation of such texts for divination, healing or the like" as well as to the literal and intellectual content (Graham 1987, 111). While explaining the process through which a text is accorded magical power, he demonstrates how people often believe written and spoken texts to have a magical quality that can be used "for purposes of divination or augury, sealing of oaths and contracts, or talismanic protection from evil or harm" (Graham 1987, 61; 58-62). Graham knows well that there is widespread reverence for physical copies of scripture among many religious communities, including Buddhists ones such as the Japanese Nichiren Sect (Graham 1987, 62-65).

Therefore, we need to examine more than the oral/aural dimension in order to understand the "folk appropriation of texts" that Graham emphasizes. Many religious communities in history had a very limited number of elites who could utilize the magical power of scriptures by reading and reciting them. Therefore Graham's explanation ultimately sheds light only on the religious elites' way of using scriptures rather than "folk appropriation." Though it is true that adherents of religions often recite or read scriptures for magical purposes, we should not miss other various ways in which lay believers have been trying to use the power of scriptures.

In her paper, "Scripture and Its Reception: A Buddhist Case" in *Rethinking Scripture*, Miriam Levering, another inheritor of Cantwell Smith, shows how religious texts are appropriated in a contemporary Buddhist convent in Taiwan. From a comparative perspective, she suggests "four fundamental modes of reception" of scriptures that are found "wherever words and texts are scriptural": first is the informative mode, which allows texts to shape one's understanding of the world; second is the transactive mode that enables people to experience the power of the ultimate by reading and reciting scripture; third is the transformative mode, which uses the power of scripture in ritual to induce an encounter with a transcendental being or a transformation of oneself; fourth is the symbolic mode, which accepts scripture itself as a symbol of the ultimate (Levering 1989, 60; 72-90). The third and fourth modes especially help Levering account for the status and power of scripture. As part of the explanation for the third one, she demonstrates that sacred words including scriptures are believed to provide power and protection, create merits, bring benefits to people, and so on. She describes the sacred status of scripture as an object of worship when she expounds the fourth mode. Levering suggests concrete examples of how the power of scriptures is ritually assumed for Buddhist soteriology. For instance, in the convent that she observes, Buddhist nuns recite and copy sutras because they believe these actions can "eliminate past negative accumulations" (Levering 1989, 73).

Though Levering seeks to show "what essentially characterizes scripture by examining all of the ways in which individuals and communities receive these words and texts" (Levering 1989, 59), she ends up mainly emphasiz-

Possession and Repetition

ing elite reception of sutras because she investigates a Taiwanese convent community. To observe Buddhists' appropriation of their scriptures in a wider context, we should pay attention to what lay persons outside the temple and convent think of and do with the texts.

In pre-modern Korea, only a few elite monks could read and copy Buddhist sutras. It was very difficult for common people to understand the early sutras, not only because they contained very specialized terms but also because they had been translated into classical Chinese from Pali and Sanskrit. Later sutras that originated in China were too difficult to be read by lay persons, most of whom were peasants. The opportunity to be educated in classical Chinese was rare, and these texts were full of philosophical, ethical, and cosmological discourses. After the invention and dissemination of easier Korean alphabets in the fifteenth century, certain people acquired translated versions of some sutras.[3] But still in ritual contexts, recitation and reading were performed only by Buddhist monks and only in the language that had first been introduced to Korea.

The studies developed by Graham and Levering center on literate religious elites. Therefore, they are not entirely successful in offering a balanced and extensive explanation on the status and roles of scriptures as Smith had suggested. Recent works by D. Max Moerman and Jacob Kinnard cover what Graham and Levering missed. In demonstrating Buddhist sutra burial rituals in early medieval Japan that were practiced in order to "forestall the decline of the Buddhist teachings and preserve the Dharma for a future age," Moerman points out that in this context "the texts were never to be recited, studied or taught." He rightly asserts "the power of sacred texts lies not only in their words and ideas but in their materiality and instrumentality as well" (Moerman 2010, 71, 87). Kinnard offers examples from medieval Indian Buddhism. He shows that a Mahayana Buddhist text "is not necessarily a book that needs to be read but can also simply be looked at and worshipped" (Kinnard 2002, 95). These two scholars successfully show that Buddhists do not necessarily have to read or recite their sutras in order to appropriate the sacred status and power of their sutras.[4]

---

3. While Japanese Buddhists began to translate sutras written and recited in Chinese into Japanese since the early twentieth century, Koreans started their translation of some important texts into colloquial Korean in the fifteenth century.

4. Though I do not treat Hindu cases in this chapter, C. Mackenzie Brown observed that "the parallels between the Buddhist and Hindu cult of the book are many" (Brown 1986, 80). There are many Hindu practices that are similar to the Korean Buddhist ones I demonstrate here, such as venerating a holy book, using it as a talisman, gifting it to others to create merit, and keeping it at home to gain benefits. But it seems that Hindu practices were influenced by Buddhist ones, rather than vice versa, considering that "book writing, and writing in general, were accepted sooner by Buddhists

Examples from Korean Buddhism will make this point clearer. It is a matter of course that many Korean monks and nuns recite and copy sutras to appropriate their sacred power and status.[5] But various ways of appropriating the power and status of sacred sutras, which do not involve reading, reciting, learning, or studying them, have been developed for Korean lay Buddhists.

Obtaining the power and status of sutras through repetition and possession

Tuladhar-Douglas (2009) shows how Buddhists appropriate the power and sacred status of sutras by repeating and reproducing them. He further develops Gombrich's argument to demonstrate Mahayana Buddhists' extension of the ritual functions of sutras by reciting, copying, and printing sutras, and by spinning cylindrical devices into which a copy of a sutra has been placed. These actions have nothing to do with the reading the contents of the texts. Tuladhar-Douglas says that it was after the introduction of writing to Buddhism that the worship of the relics of the Buddha's physical body and of the body of his teachings in written form came to be regarded as the same thing. According to him, written texts themselves came to be recognized as the "materialized" dharma of the Buddha exceeding the powers of any non-Buddhist deity and they began to be ritually worshipped just like the body of the Buddha. In the case of the *Prajnaparamita* (Perfection of Wisdom) sutra, the text itself is the source of the ritual because it includes instructions on how the book should be ritually used. Most of all, this sutra asks people to recite and write out its contents so as to bring about rapid multiplication of the manuscript. Tuladhar-Douglas describes an example of ritual recitation of "the last remaining Sanskrit Buddhist Community" in the Kathmandu Valley. After a selected sutra is worshipped, it is torn into as many pieces as the number of priests present, and each person recites the part that is given to him. In this ritual, it is impossible for a listener to understand the content of the text because many different parts are read simultaneously, creating a tumultuous din. He argues that intelligibility and meaning should be distinguished from each other and that the meaning of repeated recitations of incomprehensible mantras and *dharani*s should be found in the act of reciting itself.

---

than by Hindus" (Brown 1986, 78). See also Waghorne (2010 [2012]) and De Semini (2016).

5. Korean monks and nuns use reciting and copying sutras to stimulate experiences of the supernatural. This is similar to the Taiwanese convent case observed by Levering in which nuns read and recite sutras not only to achieve a peaceful mind but also to make their bodies "wonderfully warm" (Levering 1989, 84).

Tuladha-Douglas provides useful examples for understanding the appropriation of scripture by way of repetition. Since about 1,000 years ago, Tibetan Buddhists have been using prayer wheels, called *mani chos-khor* (Tuladhar-Douglas 2009, 265). There are similar devices, such as a rotating sutra case or library, that have been made in China, Korea and Japan. To quote Tuladhar-Douglas's description (2009, 266), "These rotating libraries are always large. Guo, translating a Sung Dynasty handbook of 1103, gives the standard height as 6.4 meters, but some were much larger.... It is octagonal in shape, and the library has handles on the outside allowing it to be rotated." Tuladhar-Douglas provides Chinese and Japanese names of this device, *lun ts'ung* and *rinzo*, but seems to be unaware of the Korean version of it. In Korea, it is called *yunjangdae*. Though he says that the Tibetan prayer wheels and the Chinese rotating sutra case are "almost certainly genetically related," he does not indicate which was made first. He just says that Schopen locates the origin of rotating sutra cases in India, and Q. Guo gives a much earlier date for the first Chinese rotating sutra case. Considering that this device is mentioned by the poet Bai Ju Yi (白居易 in Chinese, 772–846), a Chinese writer of the Tang Dynasty, I think that the Chinese rotating sutra case preceded the Tibetan one. There is, however, no clear evidence when it began to be made in Korea. A construction record of Yongmunsa temple in Yecheon, Gyeongsangbukdo Province, which seems to date from 1840, reports the *yunjangdae* of that temple was made in the twelfth century.

Tibetans put up prayer flags, *darchor* and *lungta*, in high places in order to have the wind blow the power of the text and send meritorious effects far away. Tuladhar-Douglas also mentions Chinese and Japanese tradition of printing *dharani* or sutras in great numbers for the purpose of ritual repetition rather than education or wider readership. There is "an instance of Tibetan monks carefully pressing woodblocks into the running surface of a stream" in order to maximize the repetitive effect. He even introduces recently developed methods of ritual repetition for purifying negative karma and increasing good karma, such as installing computer recitation programs, posting animated prayer wheels on the web, and downloading mantras to a hard disk or CD-ROM to have it spin at a very high speed.

Tuladhar-Douglas's work is very valuable in that it not only traces historical contexts of the ritual repetition of sutras in Mahayana Buddhism but also offers various examples including recent ones. But I would like to point out one problem that his research does not solve. Though he says, at the beginning of his article, that Buddhist sutras have been worshipped just like the Buddha relics, he does not consider the power that the simple

Figure 2.1   *Yunjangdae* in Yongmunsa temple, Yecheon, Korea. Photo: Author.

existence of sacred texts can exert. His work focuses on the ritual repetition which is only one way of ritually appropriating the power of sutras.

Tuladhar-Douglas overemphasizes the ritual repetition of sutras and also suggests an incorrect example from Korean Buddhism. He says that a full set of *Tripitaka* blocks was completed in the early eleventh century for the purpose of ritual repetition, praying for the protection of the country against the Mongols. He argues that the court made the blocks because printing sutras was a successful way to perform ritual repetition. It is true that the Goryeo Dynasty carved a *Tripitaka* of over 80,000 woodblocks in order to protect the country from the Mongols. However, in this case, printing was not the main reason for the production of the blocks. The power that Koreans intended to obtain was not expected to come from the ritual repetition of printing sutras. It was impossible to produce many copies of the full set of *Tripitaka* blocks due to their enormous quantity. The power was thought to come from their simple existence in Korea. The idea was to make the teachings of the Buddha into correct and inclusive woodblocks as perfectly as possible. The possession of the complete set of *Tripitaka* in Korea was believed to harness the power of the Buddha to protect the country from the Mongolian invasion.

The act of possessing sutras is as important as its ritual repetition for understanding Buddhists' appropriation of the sacred status and power of sutra. These two important practices of repetition and possession are clearly attested among contemporary Korean lay Buddhists.

Korean lay Buddhists' appropriation of sutras by way of repetition

One of the easiest ways of appropriating the power of a sacred text is to recite its short versions, namely *dharani* or mantra. Just as Indian Buddhists who believe in the power of sacred words of Buddhas and Bodhisattvas recite mantra and *dharani* (Levering 1989, 64), Korean lay Buddhists often recite short versions of these sacred words. Also, as I mentioned above, Korean Buddhists have set up rotating sutra cases in temples. Spinning the sutra case is believed to create as much merit as reading all the sutras in the case. Rotating this device, as Tuladhar-Douglas says, is one of the easy ways for lay Buddhists to repeat sutras. As a matter of fact, monks also use similar means of repetition. They spin prayer wheels, recite mantras, and rotate sutra cases. For both lay Buddhists and monks, these rituals are easy and efficient. However, lay Buddhists who are unable to read or recite texts rely on these easy ways more heavily than monks do.

Nonetheless, these simple ways of creating positive merit and eliminating past negative accumulations by reciting short phrases or rotating sutra cases were apparently not enough to satisfy lay Buddhists. Some temples came up with a structure called "Haeindo" for illiterate lay Buddhists. Haeindo is a labyrinth-shaped pathway on which a summary of *Huayen Ching* (*Flower Ornament Sutra*) is written. It is said to have been invented by the founder of Korean Huayen (Hwaom in Korean) school, Uisang (625–702). He designed a labyrinth-shaped pathway filled with words of the abbreviated version of *Hua-yen Ching* with the help of his mentor, Chih-yen (602–688, the second patriarch of the Chinese *Hua-yen* school). We can see the purpose of Haeindo from the notice board in the courtyard of the Haeinsa temple in Hapcheon, Gyeongsangnamdo province, which is one of the "Three Jewel Temples" of Korea.

> ... Walking through the course of Haeindo is a journey of eliminating negative karma effects and awakening to the truth. If you write your wishes down on a piece of wish-paper and walk through Haeindo, they will be fulfilled. Furthermore, if you write down penitent confessions then walk through, there will be great merit for your afterlife. When a person who has walked through Haeindo many times while alive stands before the mirror of karma after death, Haeindo will be reflected on the mirror. Then sinful karma of the person will go through the labyrinth of Haeindo. During the process, each sinful act will vanish away while passing through letters of the summary of the *Flower Ornament*

Korean Religious Texts in Iconic and Performative Rituals

Figure 2.2   *Haeindo* in Haeinsa temple, Hapcheon, Korea. Photo: Author.

> Sutra. The finishing spot after walking around the whole Haeindo is the same point as you started. This is a place of the Perfection of Wisdom (*prajnaparamita*) where you will become free from evil passions. You will be born anew with sinful karmas removed through the mercy of all Buddhas and Bodhisattvas.

According to this board, walking through the course of Haeindo results in awakening to the truth, fulfillment of wishes, elimination of sinful karma, and being born anew. Considering that the letters of the abbreviated version of the sutra eliminate sinful acts, it is manifest that the purpose of this ritual walking is to appropriate the power of the sutra. The board also articulates the effect of repeating the sutra with the mention of the salvific power that can be created by walking through the pathway "many times."

Unlike the portable prayer wheels of Tibet, we cannot say that rotating sutra cases and *Haeindo* are closely connected to the daily lives of lay Buddhists because they are available only at temples. But as Mircea Eliade argued more than sixty years ago, religious people's experiences of the sacred do not necessarily happen within temples or convents. "The dialectic of hierophany" is supposed to penetrate into the daily lives of religious persons (Eliade 1949, 446). As "*homo religiosus*" tends to put the sacred into his profane reality, sacred scriptures or their abbreviated words that are revered and recited in temples are naturally brought into the every-

Possession and Repetition

day lives of lay believers. Therefore, those who recognize sutras as sacred objects but are not capable of reading or reciting them must develop ways to appropriate their sacred power and status in their everyday lives.

In Korea, there is a tradition for devoted Buddhists to invite a monk from a nearby temple and ask him to recite specific sutras for important family events, such as rites of passage, moving, or house construction. Such recitations have been available only to wealthy lay Buddhists. But contemporary Korean lay Buddhists are enjoying a kind of democratization of recitation, thanks to the development of electronic devices and the internet. They can purchase a CD that contains recitations of sutras and play it whenever they feel a need for it. In fact, some Buddhists play CDs or tape recordings of sutras for purification of a new house or land. Recently, many internet websites have become popular among lay Buddhists who try to use free sutra recitations. They visit websites that are run not only by temples,[6] but also by private individuals. There are some sites that mainly supply Buddhist music and recitation of sutras.[7] Some other sites provide all kinds of information and contents related to Buddhism including educational materials, a Buddhist dictionary, an art gallery, cartoons, and children's stories, as well as recordings of sutras.[8]

One internet Buddhist community (internet café) has more than 16,000 members. The average number of daily visitors at this website is over 2,000 and about 500 new writings are posted every day.[9] Many Buddhists try to create positive merit by copying texts or mantras online. While one website offers its members chances to write calligraphic letters of a passage from a sutra with a computer mouse,[10] most of the other internet sites let people type parts of sutras and post them on a board titled "copying sutras board."[11] Of course, people write or type passages of sutras that are translated or transliterated into Korean. Though there have been controversies among Korean Buddhists over the efficacy of these internet means, more and more lay Buddhists are accepting them as convenient tools for appropriating the power of sutras. In sum, the internet has made lay Buddhists'

---

6. For example, Songgwangsa temple, one of the "Three Jewel Temples" of Korea runs www.songgwangsa.org and another "Jewel Temple," Tongdosa temple, runs www.tongdosa.or.kr. (accessed 24 July 2009).
7. For example, see www.sambori.com (accessed 10 August 2010).
8. For example, see www.buddhapia.com (accessed 10 August 2010).
9. I referred to http://cafe.daum.net/yumhwasil (accessed 10 August 2010).
10. I referred to www.sagyeong.net. The last time I accessed this site was November 2009, but this site was closed when I tried to access it in August 2010.
11. See http://cafe.daum.net/yumhwasil, http://cafe.daum.net/bohhyun, http://cafe.daum.net/BNet33, http://cafe.daum.net/gPdh (accessed 5 January 2010).

attempt to use the power of sutras by way of repetition much easier than before. The development of technology is extending "the dialectic of hierophany."

Korean lay Buddhists' appropriation of sutras by way of possession

Levering mentions the important role that lay Buddhists play in the Indian Buddhist publishing industry. While chanting sutras remains the most common method of cultivating and transferring merits for monks and nuns, the Buddhist publishing industry is "largely supported by lay donors planting merit by sponsoring the copying and publication of sutras" (Levering 1989, 74). In Korea also, financially underwriting the publication of sutras has been a very important way of assuming the power of sutras and creating positive merits for oneself. Many contemporary Korean Buddhists purchase complete collections of sutras just for the sake of possessing them, not for reading or studying them. When Tan-huh (1913–1983), a revered Korean Buddhist priest of high virtue and a buddhologist, translated and published collections of sutras in the 1960s and 1970s, even many illiterate Buddhists bought them for the purpose of having them. The act of possessing sutras has little to do with the actual reading and learning of their contents. Putting a nice collection of sutras on a bookshelf of one's house is believed to have the same meaning and effect as enshrining a Buddha statue in one's house. To borrow the words of Eliade again, Korean lay Buddhists' appropriation of sutras by way of possession is a good example of *homo religiosus*' attempt to realize the sacred in the profane world.

Buddhists often present a copy of sutras, especially the *Flower Ornament Sutra, Lotus Sutra, Diamond Sutra,* and *Heart Sutra,* to their cherished friends and family members. This custom is called *bupbosi (dharma dana)*, which means "giving alms of the sacred teaching." The givers think that they can plant merit by distributing the sacred words of the Buddha and that it is an excellent gift because the receiver can have the blessing and power of the Buddha by possessing the sacred text.

Splendidly decorated or gilded bronze sutras, as well as traditional book type sutras, are popular among lay Buddhists. The "Golden Heart Sutra" is one of the steadily selling products that are advertised in papers and on the internet. The internet advertisement does not directly state that good effects will be brought about by simply having the product in one's possession. Rather, it mentions the peace of mind that results from reading it. But it is clear that this gilded sutra is not made for reading at home. Very few lay Buddhists would be able to read it because the content is not translated into Korean. The marketers try to avoid violating legal restrictions against misleading and exaggerated advertisements but they still allude to the positive effects of possessing this product. For instance, by referring to it as "a household god that each Buddhist family should enshrine at home," the marketers assert that the gilded sutra has sacred power and status. The advertisement recommends this product which is "infused with the high virtue of the Buddha" especially to persons "moving to a new house, beginning a new business, praying for success in business, supporting a child preparing for an important examination, experiencing insomnia caused by wavelength from an underground water vein, suffering from misfortunes and disasters at home, or going through distress because of money problems."[12]

Not only sutras in a book form but also other goods on which words from sutras are printed or engraved attract Korean lay Buddhists. Buddhist shops serve customers with almost every kind of thing for daily use, such as stationary, tableware, tea cup sets, towels and more. In newspaper and online advertisements, I could find steadily selling products such as wristwatches with a passage from *Heart Sutra* engraved on them. Goods on which "Great *Dharani*" is printed are also very popular.[13] The text is printed on towels, tea-table cloths, wall clocks, mobile phone ornaments, purses, wallets and many other goods. The catch phrase for advertising "*Dharani* Purse" and "*Dharani* Wallet" is "Miraculous Experience of Obtaining Your Fortune and Having All of Your Wishes Fulfilled." It attracts lay Buddhists by saying that "the possession of this purse (or wallet) helps the owner fulfill any wishes, avoid disasters" and "makes money flow in from all directions."[14] The possession of these products with printed words of sutras is believed to exert the power that the Buddha can offer.

In 2007, "Seongbulhwa," which means "becoming Buddha sneakers," were released on the market. These shoes are embroidered with a mantra, "Om-Mani-Padme-Hum." Its newspaper advertisement emphasizes that the mantra on the shoes always leads people in auspicious ways and helps them avoid misfortunes.[15] It also says that by wearing these shoes "people can achieve peace of mind, have sound judgment, plant positive merit, and terminate three disasters [flood/fire/wind or war/pestilence/

---

12. http://dabosa.co.kr/shop/shopdetail.html?brandcode=001001000001&search=&sort =brandname (accessed 10 August 2010).
13. "Great *Dharani*" is a part of *Thousand Hands Sutra* which originated in China.
14. From March 2008, advertisements have been on the internet and newspapers including *Don-A Daily* and *Kum-kang-sin-mun* (*Diamond Newspaper*). Both were published in Korean.
15. The first advertisement was on *Bul-gyo-sin-mun* (*Buddhism Newspaper*), 24 October 2007, which was published in Korean.

famine]." The owner does not have to recite the mantra. He or she has only to wear the shoes to experience the miraculous power of the sacred phrase.

The commercial motives of marketers who exploit the faith of Buddhists are obviously involved in the advertisements I cited above. On the other hand, the success of these advertisements in marketing such products proves that many Korean lay Buddhists try to appropriate the power of sutras or certain parts of their sacred words by possessing them. Korean lay Buddhists have developed various ways of possessing sutras in order to assume the sacred status and power of sutras.

Conclusion

The power, status, and roles of religious scripture have not receives due attention in spite of their importance. Wilfred Cantwell Smith and his followers regard scripture as a kind of sacred words and emphasize its oral and aural dimensions to overcome the tendency of Western scholarship to focus on the contents of written texts. They have successfully brought into relief the importance of orality that had been neglected before. But if we focus only on the oral/aural dimensions, it is difficult to explain how lay persons who do not have the ability to read or recite sutras appropriate religious texts. To cover this unexplained aspect of scripture, we have to investigate various ways in which lay persons make use of scripture in their daily lives.

In this chapter, by examining examples from Korean Buddhism, I suggested two important ways in which lay Buddhists appropriate the power and status of sutras: repetition and possession. As is well known, Buddhists have developed facile ways of efficiently repeating sutras and maximizing meritorious virtues. Such ways include reciting *dharani* and mantra, which are abbreviated versions of sutras, and spinning prayer wheels. In addition, contemporary Korean lay Buddhists have come up with new means of repeatedly hearing recited sutras and copying passages of these texts on the internet. "*Bupbosi*," a tradition of giving sutras for the purpose of possession is also still practiced. Some lay Buddhists purchase fancy gilded sutras in order to do well on a college entrance examination or to increase their wealth with the help of the transcendent power of these sacred texts. Some wear shoes that are embroidered with words of a mantra to gain peace of mind and to avoid misfortunes. Korea, a country that boasts the most advanced internet technology in the world and where people advertise a purse printed with sacred words that allegedly draws money from all directions, provides excellent examples of ways for appropriating scriptures, which I expect the next five chapters will demonstrate more clearly.

3

PERFORMATIVE SCRIPTURE READING RITUALS IN EARLY KOREAN PROTESTANTISM

The Korean Protestant Church from a comparative perspective

The Korean Protestant church has grown rapidly since its introduction from the United States in the late nineteenth century. Most Korean church historians consider "the Bible study meeting" and "the revival meeting" to be among the most important factors in the church's development. Though these two phrases refer to different types of Christian meetings in contemporary Korea, originally they were the same thing. The Bible study meeting often ended in a Pentecostal experience consisting of "enthusiastic, dynamic, and charismatic" prayer and public repentance. Thus both types of meetings are often categorized under the umbrella term of "the Revival Bible Study Meeting" (Yi 2001, 98–100, 134). The fourfold increase in church membership between 1903 and 1907 that marked "the Great Revival" has often been credited to the Bible study meeting (Moffett 1962, 53).

American missionaries initiated the practice of holding Bible study meetings for educating Korean Christians, but the groups quickly came to be led by Korean lay leaders and, later, pastors. While the typical leadership of these groups changed over the years, the main part of the meetings–reading the Bible aloud–remained the same.

Little academic research has been conducted on these meetings. The Bible study meeting in early Korean Protestantism has mainly been studied in the church and in denominational seminaries, and thus it has typically been described in Christian confessional language. For example, many authors credit the results of the meetings to "the work of the Spirit of God" or "the fire of the great revival." Moffett calls the Great Revival "the white-hot, almost volcanic upheavals that shook the church in the first decade of the twentieth century." According to him, "it was a spiritual revival, explosive and spectacular, sweeping through the peninsular" and it "touched off the massive ingathering of the church." He viewed this revival as an "extraordinary manifestations of power in Korea" and compared it to the revivals of John Wesley (Moffett 1962, 52). The academic study of religion, however, should endeavor to *explain* a phenomenon rather than merely *describing* it from the perspective of those situated within specific religions. A comparative perspective can provide useful analytical tools for describing religious phenomena. As Jonathan Z. Smith has pointed out, the goal of comparison is not the act of comparison itself. Rather, comparison is a route to "explanation," "redescription," or "generalization" of that which is being compared (J. Z. Smith 2004, 29–32). Citing F. J. P. Poole, Smith suggests another rule of the comparative method: "Comparison does not deal with phenomena *in toto* or in the round, but only with an aspectual characteristic of them" (1990, 53).

In this chapter, I focus on the public reading ritual of the Bible, which constituted the main part of the Bible study meeting in early Korean Protestantism. Reading rituals provide a good aperture for framing comparisons between different traditions and cultures, as Wilfred Cantwell Smith pointed out in arguing that the dynamic functions of the Bible as scripture should be studied from the perspective of historical and comparative studies (W. C. Smith 1989). Demonstrating the performative function of public Bible reading allows the phenomenon to become an object of comparative study rather than only being described in the language of the church. In addition, we can illuminate a neglected aspect of scripture by studying the public reading ritual. As William Graham noted, even though "the spoken word of scripture has been overwhelmingly the most important medium through which religious persons and groups throughout history have known and interacted with scriptural texts," the academic study of the Bible and other sacred scripture has failed to sufficiently emphasize its oral aspects (Graham 1987, 155, 157–159). In particular, Protestant Christian scholarship often neglects the oral function of the Bible. Focusing on the public *reading* rituals of the Bible study meeting underscores the importance of the oral uses of the Bible.

In this chapter, I address two issues in the performative dimension of scriptures evident in the Korean Bible study meeting. First, I offer an explanation for why Bible readings promoted the conversion of Koreans to Christianity in the particular ethos of traditional Korean culture. Bible readings in early Korean Protestantism facilitated the absorption of Christianity into Korean culture by accommodating traditional religious practices and by offering a way for native Koreans to play active roles in the newly introduced Christianity. Second, I will provide a theoretical clarification of the meaning of "performative" in the theory of a "performative dimension" of scripture. James W. Watts proposes a three-dimensional model of scriptures as consisting of textual, performative, and iconic dimensions (2006 [2008], 135-159). He argues that religious communities ritualize scriptures along these three dimensions. I add that scripture readings are performative in J. L. Austin's sense of performative speech as shown by their effect on the rapid growth of early Korean Protestantism. Austin wrote (1962, 6): "... to utter the sentence (in, of course, the appropriate circumstances) is not to *describe* my doing of what I should be said in so uttering to be doing or to state that I am doing it: it is to do it" (emphasis Austin's). The necessary conditions of performative utterances, which are stipulated by Austin, are fulfilled through ritualizing the activity of reading and ritualizing the Bible itself. By comparing Korean Bible readings with the language of African healing rituals and applying several important ritual theories to the Korean readings, I will demonstrate how the Bible readings operate as performative utterances. But before embarking on a historical and theoretical explanation of the Korean Bible study meetings, I will first introduce and briefly describe these meetings.

The Bible study meeting in early Korean Protestantism

Though each Korean Protestant denomination explains the early Bible study meetings somewhat differently, most church historians agree that this type of meeting developed from the Bible education programs of the missionary William B. Scranton in 1888 and the missionary Horace G. Underwood in 1890 ("The Revival Bible Study Meeting and Church" 2006). By 1900, the meeting was formalized as an annual or biannual special event and became an essential feature of the Korean Protestant church. According to the missionary report of 1904, about 60 percent of Korean Protestant Christians participated in Bible study meetings. By 1909, more than 800 Bible study meetings were held in the missionary district of the American Presbyterian Church alone (Gwangsu Kim 1996, 293).[1] Most issues of Christian newspapers from this time include notices describing when and where Bible study meetings would be held, as well as testifying that the meetings of certain local churches had ended successfully. The size of the meetings varied: in small local churches the meetings could involve as few as five participants, but large urban churches might host meetings attended by around six hundred Christians from all over the province. The

---

1. Several Western Protestant denominations, including American, Australian, and Canadian Presbyterians and Methodists, divided up missionary districts of Korea and took the responsibility for the mission work of the district in charge. For a map of the missionary districts in the early twentieth-century Korea, see http://www.kukminilbo.co.kr/missiontoday/c_history/root/roottxt14.html.

meetings, which usually lasted from seven to ten days, were typically held during the winter when the peasants and farmers had more free time from their work. People who traveled long distances carried portable equipment for cooking on the road and lodged together in church buildings. Others who were lucky enough to have relatives close to the church could stay with them (S. F. Moore 1906; Gwangsu Kim 1996, 293).

Church historians agree that "the revival movement began from a Bible study meeting held by missionaries in Wonsan" (*The History of 70 Years of the Saemunan Church* 1958, 43) and that the Pyeong-An province Bible study meeting that was held at Pyongyang Changdaehyeon Presbyterian in 1907 marked the climax of the Great Revival (Insu Kim 2002, 246). In the words of Min, "the wave of the revival rushed on in a vast expanse by the influence of the Bible study meeting" (Min 1993, 267). They also maintain that Bible study meetings in the early Korean church became the background of the early revival movement because the meetings provide Koreans with chances to experience the Holy Spirit and achieve a kind of spiritual power (Gwangsu Kim 1996, 293). Moffett claims that the Great Revival began when a Western missionary confessed his sins during a Bible study meeting.

> The revival began quietly enough in a week of prayer and Bible study for missionaries in Wonsan, led by a Methodist physician from Canada, R. A. Hardie. In the course of his Bible studies, Dr. Hardie felt compelled by the Spirit to go before his fellow missionaries and later before a Korean congregation to confess... "my own pride, hardness of heart and lack of faith..." From Wonsan revivalism spread and reached its climax at a great evening meeting in Pyongyang, in 1907. (Moffett 1962, 52–53)

In early Korean Protestantism, the confession of sins was regarded as a sign of the work of the Spirit (The Institute for Korean Church History 1989, 268–273). Christians often confessed their sins in public. After or even during the Bible study meetings, people would rise and say that "in listening to the Word" they saw their sins as they had not seen them before. Participants in the meetings felt that hearing such confessions strengthened their faith and led many non-Christians who had been invited to the meetings to convert. The Bible study meetings are therefore considered to be responsible for the Great Revival and the subsequent rapid growth of Korean Protestant church (S. F. Moore 1906).

In paying attention to the central role of the Bible in the meetings, some church historians have criticized the loss of the Bible-centered tradition as meetings transformed from Bible study to revivalism. This transformation began in the 1960s and turned into a kind of Pentecostal movement (Gwangsu Kim 1996, 293; "The Revival Bible Study Meeting and Church" 2006). Not a few ministers and lay leaders of conservative denominations express nostalgia for what they see as a gentler way of revival that emphasizes studying the Bible over fervent Pentecostal style.

Above all, it should be pointed out that the phrase "Bible study" meant something different in the meetings of the late nineteenth and early twentieth centuries in Korea than in the contemporary Christian world. "Studying" meant reading the scripture as well as the process of teaching and learning about the scripture. The early Korean Protestants expected to "receive divine grace while they were reading the Bible" (Gwangsu Kim 1996, 293). A small-scale Bible study meeting was a public reading ritual in which the Bible was read all through the service. In larger meetings, the public scripture reading formed an important part of a complex service that included singing hymns, public prayers, and the Bible study. Usually, the Bible study consisted of two parts in large meetings. First, selected chapters and books from the Bible were read or recited aloud. Then, an interpretation or explanation of the texts was given by a renowned pastor. According to S. F. Moore, who was the pastor of the Seoul Seung-Dong Church, at a series of Bible study meetings that were held in Seoul in January 1906, "one feature which seemed helpful was the repetition of Scripture by the congregation. Many precious texts were repeated line by line after the leader" (S. F. Moore 1906). The New Testament was more often read than the Old Testament. The four Gospels, the epistles of Paul, and the First Epistle of John were especially widely read (Gwangsu Kim 1996, 293; Insu Kim 2002, 247).

The Korean contexts of Bible study: Reading aloud in the Korean language

Two elements in the early Korean Protestant church seem to have influenced the development of the public reading ritual as the primary focus of studying the Bible. First, the way of studying the Bible through reading it aloud seems to have been influenced by "the Nevius Method Mission Work," which was a central principle of Korean Protestant mission work and which is believed to have been greatly helpful to the growth of the Korean Protestant Church (Insu Kim 2002, 193). John L. Nevius (1829-1893), a missionary to China for 40 years, visited Korea in 1893 and led seminars about strategies and methods for doing missionary work in Korea. After the seminars, he and other missionaries in Korea formulated "the Nevius Method of Mission Work," whose five major principles were: Bible study, self-propagation, self-government, self-support, and missionary itineration (Clark 1930; Moffett 1962, 59-61). The Nevius Method insisted that the Bible had to be the focus of all missionary work. It also emphasized the "voluntary system," in which every Korean Christian was encouraged to become a Bible teacher for others. Christians were supposed to study the Bible under the guidance of lay "helpers" and "leaders" who took "Bible Classes" led by missionaries and pastors. Each church organized small-group Bible study meetings that were led by these lay leaders.[2] Many of them did not have enough training to teach and explain the texts in detail, so it was natural that they led their Bible studies primarily by reading the texts aloud. The Bible classes of the local churches contributed to the general enthusiasm among Korean Protestants for studying the Bible and thus the Bible study meeting spread across the whole country (Gwangsu Kim 1996, 293).

The second element in the early Korean church that facilitated the spread of public Bible readings as a central ritual was the continuity between these public readings and other traditional religious practices. The traditional Korean way of studying books, especially the Confucian classical canon and the Buddhist Scriptures, involved reading through the text and reciting it. Yi explains that this was the reason reading and reciting could become the main way of studying the Bible:

> The Dawn Prayer Meeting and the Bible study meeting were the major factors of the revival movement. These were the native religious activities that had been produced in the peculiar situation of Korea... The Bible study meeting adopted the existing East Asian way of studying scriptures. *The study began by reading through the Bible, and the reading itself, rather than the interpretation, was emphasized.* (Yi 1995, 509, emphasis added)

What early Korean Christians called "study" was a public reading ritual in which texts from the Bible were read aloud.

Bible readings thus seem to have facilitated the absorption of Christianity into Korean culture by applying older Korean religious practices and by providing an avenue for Koreans rather than missionaries to take the lead in the new religion. The use of the Korean language was another important factor in Koreans accepting Christianity. If an invited Western pastor did not have a command of Korean and preached through interpreters in revival services, he could not move the Korean congregation easily, no matter how famous he might be. By contrast, if a Western missionary could speak Korean very fluently, Korean participants in his revival ser-

---

2. These Korean lay leaders played an essential part in the growth of the early Korean Protestantism. J. Z. Moore (1907), the pastor in charge of the West Circuit of the Pyongyang District, claimed, "No report of the year's work would be complete without a word as to the 'unpaid helpers.' Just how much they have contributed to the success of the past year's work will never be known, but one is safe in saying, had it not been for the faithful and enthusiastic work of the laymen, most without office and all without salary, many pages of this year's report could not have been written."

vice reacted ardently (Yi 2001, 92, 109). Therefore Protestantism, which from its origins emphasized and celebrated vernacular translations of the Bible, could grow more rapidly than the Roman Catholicism that came into Korea a century earlier but still used the Latin mass. Though it was certain that missionaries had authority over the semantic dimension of Christian scripture (see Watts 2006 [2008], for whom the semantic dimension involves "the meaning of what is written, and thus includes all aspects of interpretation and commentary as well as appeals to the text's contents in preaching and other forms of persuasive rhetoric"), public readings of the Bible in Korean translation naturally placed Korean readers in a superior position of mastery in comparison with the foreign missionaries whose fluency in the Korean language could never match their own. Native Koreans, including lay leaders and volunteer helpers, could play key roles in the newly accepted religion and contribute to its establishment in the country. Public reading did not require the interpretative expertise that was needed for textual studies. Rather, it was the ability to read Korean translations of the Bible well that was more important for the purposes of the Bible study meetings in the Korean context.

The performative force of ritual languages and the ritualization of the text

Graham has noted that Muslims regard the Arabic words read in and recited from the Qur'an to be sacred and to be endowed with a special virtue (1987, 104). Similarly, the words of the Bible when they are read in Korean translation also have a special virtue for those Koreans who read and hear them. This special quality can be described as the "performative force" of the scriptures. The example of Korean Bible reading rituals can help clarify the theoretical meaning of "performative" when used to describe the function of scriptures.

Scripture reading or recitation achieves its performative force through the ritualization of both the performance of reading and the scripture itself. In my analysis of this phenomenon in the Korean Protestant context, I follow the model of J. L. Austin who argues that a performative utterance can work only under "the appropriate circumstances." That is, "the necessary conditions" of a performative utterance are satisfied through a ritual process (Austin 1962, 13-14). These necessary conditions that must be satisfied for smooth or "happy" functioning of a performative utterance were all fulfilled in early Korean Protestantism. Austin's model follows several steps: First, Austin asserts that a conventional procedure must be accepted (1962, 14). In Korea, this was the official ritual of the Bible study meeting. Reading the Bible was the main part of the officially recognized and accepted ritual of early Korean Protestantism. Austin's second condition is that appropriate persons and circumstances for the invocation of the particular procedure are needed for the effective functioning of a performative speech. Leaders of the Bible study meeting were surely "appropriate" persons because they were famous pastors or lay leaders officially designated by churches. Third, the procedure should be executed correctly and completely by all participants. Early Korean Protestants agreed that reading the scripture was an appropriate procedure for receiving the sacred words. The Bible study meeting was regarded as a special sort of worship service, thus an official ritual, in which accuracy was important. Correct and complete reading or recitation of sections of the Bible was necessary for the public reading ritual, since most early Korean Protestants believed in the "verbal inspiration" of the Bible. Austin's fourth condition is that the participants should have the intention to conduct themselves in accordance with the ritual and should actually do so (1962, 15). The participants in the Bible study meetings vowed to follow the teachings of the Bible. They intended to conduct themselves in accordance with what was uttered and they really tried to do so.

The words in Austin's examples of performative utterances related in a straightforward manner to the action they perform, but that is not always so in Korean Bible reading rituals. Many Korean Christians testify that their Bible reading results in positive effects which are not directly related to the contents of the text they read. To demonstrate that words of performative utterances do not always correspond to actions they perform, I will review some cases of "meeting for reading through the entire Bible," which took place among Korean Protestant Christians in the early 2000s.[3] This meeting is usually held for four to seven days, during which participants concentrate on reading the Bible. While some Korean Protestants participate in this meeting to understand the contents of the Bible intellectually, some obviously expect to experience the performative power of reading the Bible in a ritual context. The following quotation is taken from a Korean church's promotional material for a meeting for reading through the Bible.

---

3. It should be also noted that often these meetings aim to fulfill Austin's third necessary condition, the correct and complete procedure, by using audio files, CDs, or cassette tape recordings of the Bible. Some meetings have participants listen and repeat the recordings in low voices, or just read with their eyes following the sound, lest participants who have read the Bible for several consecutive days should have difficulty in concentrating due to the fatigue and should read the Bible incorrectly. http://www.3927ok.com/index2.htm (27/12/2007). Some Korean Christians believe that there are those who are especially gifted in reading the Bible who are able to provide listeners with strong inspiration. It is said that their reading of the Bible is recorded to protect their vocal cords from being damaged by frequent use. http://www.ezrahouse.org/tape/cd_desc_07a.htm (27/12/2007).

We will read through the word of God during the four days of the Jesus festival of our church, training ourselves in reading the Bible. During this short period of four days, while you read through the Bible, you will experience a joy and delight that you have never had before, along with the tremendous power of the word of God. The Bible says, "the Word was God" (John 1:1). ... We usually invite a famous lecturer of the Bible to hear the word of God during the summer Jesus festival. However, it is obvious that reading through the entire Bible in this time of beginning a new year is incomparably more valuable than a good lecturer's teaching. There is nothing better in the world than beginning a new year by reading through the entire Bible, because the word of God is God himself! Those who read through the entire Bible testify as following:

"I feel like a new person because I have deep impressions and great joy!"
(Psalm 119: 74)
"The word of God becomes sweeter than honey to my mouth."
(Psalm 119: 103)
"Diseases of our souls and bodies are treated."
(Hebrew 4: 12-13)
"Stupid minds are changed into geniuses."
(Psalm 119: 98-100)
"Your wish for the year will be fulfilled [just as mine was]."
(Psalm 103: 5)

... Please prepare by praying from now that you will be able to participate in the meeting. This meeting for reading through the entire Bible will completely change your life. We will fast mornings and read the Bible till midnight.[4]

There are several points in this quotation that should draw the attention of scholars of comparative religion. It articulates the ritual significance of the New Year's Day and relates it to the meeting for reading through the entire Bible. Furthermore, we can verify the iconic dimension of scripture here, in its identification of the Bible with God himself. The semantic dimension is also ritualized when testifiers specify the texts by chapter and verse that they believe support their miraculous experiences.

However, for the theme of this chapter, I would like to pay more attention to the performative dimension that is confirmed in these testimo-

---

4. http://mid.or.kr/board/list_detail.asp?board=freeboard&no=109&step=0&reno=0&nowpage=26 (8/12/2007). Though most propagating materials of the meetings for reading through the entire Bible mention the performative work of reading the Bible, I cite this promotional material because it emphasizes the dimension more strongly than others and includes important points that I want to stress in this chapter. There are also personal blog posts in which individual Christians who have participated in the meeting testify to their experiences similarly to the quoted testimonies. For instance, see http://blog.ohmynews.com/pretty645/131062 (30/5/2008).

nies, in which the mystical power of the Bible is believed to be exercised by reading it. One participant stated that they became a better person and a better Christian, which is not manifestly related to what they read. More surprisingly, some testify that their diseases were treated, that they became smarter, and that their New Year's wish was fulfilled, simply because they read through the entire Bible and not any specific texts that may be related to their miraculous experiences. Since reading through the entire Bible performs some things that are not directly related to most of the contents of the Bible, we find a case that clearly differs from Austin's description of a performative utterance.

Anthropological studies of ritual language press the case for expanding the range and nature of performative language that Austin described, by providing examples that show how some utterances work and obtain results that do not correspond to their contents. Since this point may not be an obvious one, I will summarize some of this research in some detail before returning to Korean Bible Study meetings. In "Discourse about Difference: Understanding African Ritual Language," B. C. Ray summarizes and compares the works of two anthropologists, Edith Turner and Paul Stoller. They document the "performative force" of African ritual language, which Ray defines as "how ritual words make things happen in people's lives" (Ray 2000, 102). Turner deals with the *ihamba* healing rite of an Ndembu village (1992, 138–179) and Stoller describes the efficacy of ritual language that is used in the sorcerer's healing rituals among the *Songhay* of Niger (Stoller and Olkes 1987, 69–70, 153). The Ndembu people have few myths or cosmological narratives for recitation in the healing ritual (Turner 1969, 14), though the recitation of cosmological myths has commonly been regarded as a characteristic feature of so-called "archaic" or "primitive" religions (Eliade 1957, 80–85). The participants of the *ihamba* instead utter aloud their personal grudges and feelings of anger both toward each other and toward the suffering patient, and the patient too expresses her anger and resentment. The words of the participants are regarded as the active agent in the process and of prime importance to the success of the *ihamba* ritual. With singing, dancing, and drumming, the speaking participants experience "a kind of collective Pentecost experience," and the illness of the patient is believed to be removed (Ray 2000, 108).

In contrast to the Ndembu, the Songhay described by Stoller rely on a sorcerer who uses a mythic text for the healing ritual. He recites the myth three times over a gourd that contains a mixture of twigs, perfume, and water. The contents of the recited myth constitute the power of the *Songhay* ancestors and the world of sorcery. This myth is sung to Ndebbi, the intermediary between human beings and *Iri Koy*, the High God of the *Songhay* cosmos. The water in the gourd, which is now thought to contain the force of the heavens embodied in these words, is used to wash the patient. The lost spiritual double of the patient is believed to join the patient again through this healing ritual (Ray 2000, 113).

I would argue that the Ndembu's unscripted utterance of spontaneous ritual language stands in contrast to the *Songhay*'s employment of the traditional myth in its scripted ritual form. The Ndembu participants speak angry words whose contents are not prescribed in the ritual. Their words are uttered both collectively and ritually, in the context of a larger ritual that includes drumming and dancing. The *Songhay* sorcerer, on the other hand, uses the fixed form of a traditional myth, whose recitation becomes the medicine. These two rituals, however, also manifest an important similarity in that the ritual words themselves perform healing acts in both cases. As Ray argues, "What Turner has succeeded in showing us is the performative power of ritual language, its ability to rearrange people's feelings and command psychological forces to make things happen in people's lives" (Ray 2000, 110) whereas

> Stoller's account shows that, as in the Ndembu ceremony, the efficacy of the ritual consists in linking together sacred words with the spirit world and the patient's psychological state. Uttering the words had the desired effect of joining together the patient and his spiritual double... In both cases the performative force of words brought about a transformation within the suffering patient.
>
> (Ray 2000, 113)

Both African tribal healing rituals assume the power of words to heal the patients. Ray (2000, 114) argues that Austin's performative force, which is the ability of words not only to say things but also to "do" things, comes into play in these rituals. It can be said that the words of African healers perform something. They are therefore performative utterances in Austin's sense that a performative sentence does what a person is doing rather than describes or state it. African ritual languages, however, have a more complicated structure than simple performative sentences. In Austin's performative, the meaning of the speech is what is performed. For instance, when a person says, "I name this ship the Queen Elizabeth" in a launching ceremony, the act of naming is done (Austin 1962, 5). In African healing rituals, on the other hand, the ritual languages are not doing what is uttered. Rather, the words are believed to persuade or force the spirits and ailments troubling patients to go out of them. So the words do not have to include explicit indications that the goal is healing. Instead, they perform healing by threatening and soothing the spirits.

Despite this difference, Ray is correct that Austin's theory of performative utterances can explain the use of ritual language, and so it also explains the function of the performative dimension of scriptures in Korean Bible reading rituals. Scripture readings are "performative" in Austin's sense of performative speech because they do certain work. Bible readings led to the conversion of many Koreans to Christianity, as well as strengthening the faith of those who were already Christian.

Obviously, the mechanics of ritual languages in African healing rituals are different from those of Korean Bible study meetings.[5] First, the words uttered in Bible study meetings persuaded people, not spirits, and as a result, the people did what the words explicitly told them to do. Stories in the Bible wielded rhetorical power. When Korean Christians read and heard that Jesus fed five thousand people, they were amazed at the power and love of Jesus and came to rely more on Jesus. While this example shows the workings of Watts's semantic dimension of scripture that reinforces the persuasive rhetoric of preachers, it also demonstrates the performative dimension in that it involved the performance of what is written and that it really performed what is written. In addition, there are cases in which contents of the Bible that were read and heard in meetings were then literally carried out. When Korean Christians read and hear, "Love each other" (John 13: 34), they repented of not loving each other, decided to love each other, and did endeavor to show love to each other. When Korean Christians read and heard, "You are Christ's body and individually members of it" (1 Corinthians 12: 27) in a meeting held in Pyongyang, they also repented of not loving their fellows and believed that they had been made into the one body of Jesus. The words commonly used in Christian healings in early Korean Protestantism also contrast with the African healing ritual languages. Some pastors shouted to bodily or mentally sick persons, "In the name of Jesus Christ, I command you to come out of her (or him)!" and there are many reports that attest to the efficacy of the words. Unlike the African cases, however, the meaning of the words uttered applies directly to the ritual being performed.

Technically, the verbal form of these commands and exhortations are not performative utterances in Austin's sense any more than the African ritual languages are. They call on the audience to act in particular ways, but the language does not itself perform the action it commands. It is the

---

5. As Jonathan Z. Smith points out, comparison has to catch out differences, as well as similarities (1990, 47). There are more differences that should be noted. For example, the aim of the performance in Korea is different; words are uttered in order to study the Bible, rather than for the purpose of healing a malady. In addition, the performance takes different forms. In Korean Bible study meetings, the utterance is performed mainly through reading the written text, while reading is not found in the African examples.

context in a reading of a sacred text that lends them a performative quality, in Austin's sense. Whereas in another context, the exhortations of an ancient text from a foreign culture are unlikely to arouse in readers anything more than curiosity, the Bible study meetings made readers and hearers feel that they were themselves directly addressed by the text. The ritual setting lent the words performative power.

Even if the scripture was read outside the context of a Bible study meeting, the believers' scripture readings still would have met the conditions of performative utterances because the religious text is officially accepted and believers respect its authority. Reading the Bible is a ritualized act. The scripture reading of believers is different from their reading of a newspaper. When a believer reads the Bible, the reading is not an ordinary act of reading because reading the Bible is a deeply meaningful practice for believers. Thus, as reading scripture is differentiated from a believer's ordinary activity of reading, it becomes "ritualized" (Bell 1992, 92; see also Bell 1997, 138-139). In addition, the religious authority of the Bible for believers promotes the ritualization of the act of reading scripture. As Catherine Bell asserts, "ritualization is a way of acting that tends to promote the authority of forces deemed to derive from beyond the immediate situation" (Bell 1997, 82). The necessary conditions for the effective functioning of performative utterances could be more strongly fulfilled in the official ritual of the Bible study meeting because in that context scripture reading was ritualized even more. The uttered words were effective in promoting conversions to Christianity and strengthening the faith of believers.

To understand the performative force of such scripture readings for early Korean Protestants, we must go beyond Austin's theory of performative words to consider the performative power of words within rituals. Ninian Smart points out that ritual is important in religion because it functions performatively just as words and gestures do (2000, 117). Some anthropologists have also paid attention to the creative power of ritual itself, in addition to the performative force of its words. Theorists of ritual practice, including Bell (1997, 82), stress that ritual encompasses a set of activities that construct cultural patterns as well as express them. Roy Rappaport more persuasively articulates the performative force of ritual. He asserts that ritual has creative functions in two different senses: not only does ritual inform participants of symbolic meanings, it also sometimes transforms the participants and/or their surroundings (Rappaport 1999, 109-114). He uses the dubbing ritual as an example. Dubbing does not instruct a youth to be a knight, nor does it let him know how to be a knight. Rather, "it makes him a knight." Following Austin, Rappaport calls this dynamic the "performative" force of ritual. To perform ritual is not only "to conform to its order" but also "to make it substantial" (1999, 125). Thus ritual not only represents the symbolic meanings inherent in myth and doctrine, but it also locates willing participants in relation to those meanings. Through ritual, participants index themselves within the "canonical" order represented by the event (Rappaport 1999, 15, 54–58).

In the Korean Bible study meetings, the contents of the read words was given performative force by the ritualization of the reading experience and the ritualization of the Bible itself. In Rappaport's terms, the ritual indexed the participants as directly addressed by the text and many of them responded by accepting this new identity through conversion to Christianity or by recommitment to the faith. Public confession modeled this indexical function of the Bible study meetings by making explicit their acceptance of a Christian identity. Thus the force of the scripture's words gained performative force because the words were uttered in a ritual context and thus are ritualized. The ritualized words used at the Bible study meetings achieve their performative force with the help of ritual.

The possibility of further comparisons

the Korean Bible study meeting has previously been described mainly within a Protestant perspective as "that which caused the Great Revival of Holy Sprit by teaching the way of the Holy Spirit" (Min 1993, 269). By using a comparative perspective, however, the study of religion can "redescribe" these meetings and thus provide theoretical explanations of Korean Protestant rituals that are differentiated from those of Church historians. Jonathan Z. Smith argues that the purpose of comparative study is "redescription" of the exempla and the "rectification" of academic categories (2004, 29). Such analysis therefore does not treat Korean Bible study meetings as distinctive religious miracles, as scholars within the church might see them, but rather as phenomena for academic study from the perspective of comparative religion. Smith also points out that scholars of religion have to seek generalization, rather than specification or universalization, for theoretical research. "Generalization is understood to be a mental, comparative, taxonomic activity that directs attention to co-occurrences of selected stipulated characteristics while ignoring others" (2004, 369). I have redescribed the Bible study meeting by focusing on the participants' use of ritualized language and performance, which are readily generalizable characteristics of the meetings.

As a result, I have been able at the historical level to show the specifically Korean cultural context of the Bible study meeting. I emphasized the role of the Korean lay leaders and volunteers in early Korean Protestantism. Reading translated scripture made it possible for native Koreans to play leading roles in the church. Additionally, the continuity in Korean religious culture from reading Confucianism and Buddhist scriptures to reading the Bible in the study meetings was demonstrated. At the theoretical level, investigation of the Korean Bible Study meetings led to clarification of the meaning of "performative." Scripture readings are performative in J. L. Austin's sense of a performative utterance. Austin's necessary conditions for performative speech were satisfied through the ritualization of the activity of reading the Bible. Roy Rappaport's elucidation of the indexical role of ritual made possible a more precise description of the relationship between the words of scripture and their effects on hearers. The public scripture readings gained performative force because both the reading and the scripture itself were ritualized. The ritual indexed participants as the intended audience of these words and their acceptance of that identity produced conversion to or confirmation of faith. Thus the read or recited words from the Bible functioned performatively to bring about Koreans' conversions to Christianity and/or to strengthen their Christian faith.

In order to understand and explain the effects of the Korean Bible study meetings, comparable religious phenomena concerned with the performative force of ritual language were ferreted out from various cultures. In this chapter, I have not hesitated to compare this Korean ritual with African healing rituals. Comparison does not have to be limited to spatio-temporal contiguities or genealogical linkage, as long as we impose strict criteria on the kinds of things we can compare (Jonathan Z. Smith 2004, 14, 368). More cases for comparison will be able to shed light on the various ways in which reading scripture can function with performative force (see Graham 1987).

One fruitful area for further comparison would be between the Korean Bible study meetings and ancient Jewish and early Christian reading practices. For example, Watts asserts that "the majority of the Hebrew Bible's references to reading law describe a public reading of an entire legal document" (1999, 15). Not only Moses and his successor Joshua, but also Josiah and Ezra dedicate several days to public readings of the law book. The form and effect of Ezra's public reading ritual are very similar to those of the Korean Bible study meeting: "They read from the book, from the law of God, with interpretation" (Nehemiah 8: 8). In these cases from the Hebrew Bible, the performative force of ritual language, along with many other element, of course, can explain the effectiveness of the ritual. Through the solemn atmosphere of religious ritual, the conditions for the performative force of the uttered text must have been satisfied. More examples of reading scripture in ritual contexts from various cultures can be expected to confirm the performative power of such rituals.

4

SENSORY READINGS OF SCRIPTURES BY NEO-CONFUCIAN SCHOLARS

A new perspective on Neo-Confucian readings of scriptures

Studies of Confucian "scriptures" have been exclusively focused on their content, especially on their philosophical and ideological aspects, just like most other studies of religious scriptures. However, some scholars in relatively recent years have tried to overcome the imbalanced tendency of Western scholarship to be occupied with the content of scripture (Smith 1971; Graham 1987; Watts 2006 [2008]; Yoo 2010 [2012], revised as Chapter 2 above). Wilfred Cantwell Smith, who first pointed out this imbalance, argued that scholars of academic studies of religion should treat scripture as "a living force in the life" of religious people and should pay attention to what people do with scripture (Smith 1971). Agreeing with Smith, I will demonstrate in this chapter how Confucian scholars try to make the most of scriptures by making sensory images in reading them, while putting to one side traditional Confucian subjects involving abstract concepts or philosophical discourses.

I would like to emphasize that the term "scripture" is very adequate to designate Confucian classical texts, although some may doubt if the term "scripture" is appropriate in the Confucian context. First of all, as Rodney Taylor correctly points out, Confucian books that are linked to the tradition of the sage, who "hears the Way of Heaven and manifests it to the world" (Taylor 1990, 32), can be described as the scriptures of Confucianism.[1] According to Taylor, the Five Classics are "the repository of

---

1. This is the reason Taylor even regards those Confucian books as "holy books" (Taylor 1990, 23). It should be noted that the Chinese word 聖人, which is usually translated "the sage" in English, can be literally translated as "the sacred person." As mentioned above, the sage was the person who could hear and manifest the will of Heaven. Among sages, Confucian scholars have counted Confucius and some ancient rulers in the classical texts, including the Three Sovereigns and the Five Emperors whom

such manifestations" (Taylor 1990, 32), and the Four Books were thought to represent "the quintessential expression of *li* (理)" (Taylor 1990, 35), which designates principle or truth. Secondly, it should be noted that the Chinese word *ching* (經), which labels the "Classics" of Confucianism, has also been used for the Buddhist sutras and relatively recently for the Christian Bible, which are generally accepted as religious scriptures.

Here I will pay particular attention to the reading method suggested by Chu Hsi (1130–1200) of China and Yi Hwang (pen name Toegye, 1501–1570) of Korea, leading scholars of the Neo-Confucian school of the two countries. Both of them were confident that sensory reading of scriptures enabled scholars to have a kind of religious experience in which they could see the sages and hear their voices. As S. Brent Plate reminds us, "there is no thinking without first sensing" and "the primary contact points between the self and the world" are the five sense organs (Plate 2014, 5, 7). It is through the senses that human beings become and remain conscious of objects, and even embody consciousness. Experience associated with religion is also only possible through the senses. Mircea Eliade points out that "broadly speaking, there can be no religious experience without the intervention of the senses. ... Throughout religious history, sensory activity has been used as a means of participating in the sacred and attaining to the divine" (Eliade 1960, 74). Confucian scholars tried to appropriate their senses to contact the sage, or the sacred person, through scriptures, just like shamans who try to connect to the sacred through their "strangely sharpened sense" (Eliade 1960, 81).

In reading scriptures, Neo-Confucian scholars of China and Korea made a practice of mobilizing all available senses by using several parts of their bodies at the same time. They were encouraged to see texts with their eyes, recite them by mouth, hear the voice of their recitation by ear, and often copy the texts with their hands. Furthermore, they tried to commune with the sages and fully internalize their teachings through their senses of sight, hearing, and taste, though in their imagination rather than appealing directly to the physical senses. They visualized the image of the sage, the author of the text, and the wise men who are disciples and discussants of the sage. That is, Neo-Confucian scholars imagined they were seeing sages and wise men teach them right on the spot as they were reading. In addition, scholars tried to auralize the voices of sages and wise men, imagining they were hearing their voices when they were hearing their own voices reading, often along those of their colleagues when several

---

many contemporary scholars think to have been ancient deities (Küng and Ching 1989, 10), and the three founders of the Chou dynasty.

scholars read together. Scholars also loved to compare reading to eating and understanding texts to tasting them, often saying that they were feeling the "taste" of scriptures. Such comparisons were made very often, vividly, and in detail. However, it was not just comparison or metaphor. The scholars created the sensory images of tasting when they were reading, and they imagined they were eating the text. Their "religious experience," in which they thought that they saw and heard the sage and tasted scriptures, depended on their "sensory experience" and "sensory activity" (Eliade 1960, 81). The starting point was their own voices reading, which soon came to be heard as the voice of the sage. Neo-Confucian scholars had "a sensitivity that can perceive and integrate these new experience" (Eliade 1960, 81).

Confucian practices of visualization and auralization in reading have not drawn the attention of scholars.[2] Though some studies allude to these practices, it is difficult to find works that focus on sensory readings in Neo-Confucianism. Daniel Gardner points out that Chu advised Confucian readers to make scripture their own in Chu's "Methods of Reading," which corresponds to the tenth and eleventh chapters of his *Classified Conversations*. He briefly introduces Chu's comparison of meditative reading to savoring the flavor and Chu's suggestion that readers of the sages' texts should try to "speak with them face to face" (Gardner 2004, 112). However, Gardner does not articulate the role of the senses in Neo-Confucian reading, though he knows that Chu asked readers to make visual, auditory, and gustatory imagery.

Neo-Confucian readings of scripture, as emphasized by Chu and Yi, began with readers' senses in that they first saw the text and heard their own

---

2. For instance, the entry "Visualization" in the *Encyclopedia of Religion* says only "See Buddhism, Schools of; Daoism; Meditation" (Jones 2005, 9627). In contrast, scholars of Buddhism have discussed visualization practices in reciting sutras, which include envisioning "a buddha or bodhisattvas as a kind of visualized icon to worship or receive teachings" (McMahan 2010; see also Gregory 1986; Yamabe 1999; Hennessey 2011). The influence of Buddhism and Daoism on Chu Hsi is manifest, though he often criticized them and tried to show the Confucianism is superior (Ching 2000, 152–188). Considering that his doctrine and methods of self-cultivation were undoubtedly affected by Buddhism and Daoism, his suggestions on reading also seem to have something to do with them. However, we should not rush to a conclusion that neo-Confucian visualization was formed under the influence of Buddhism and Daoism. Visualizing the deities or ancestors in ritual contexts also appears in some early Confucian texts including the *Book of Rites* and the *Analects*. According to "Significance of Sacrifice" in the *Book of Rites*, "In sacrificing, King Wen served the dead in the same way he served the living. … When he mentioned his father' name, he did as if he saw him" (24.008). And the *Analects* attests that "[Confucius] offered sacrifice to his ancestors as if his ancestors were actually there and offered sacrifice to gods as if the gods were actually there" (3.12).

voices reading. Furthermore, they thought they saw the sages, authors and characters of scripture, heard their voices, and tasted the flavor of scripture. Though they did not see and hear the sages directly or physically, and though they did not literally chew and eat the books, their readings really involved the senses of seeing, hearing, and tasting. As David Morgan persuasively argues, seeing is not limited to direct and physical seeing but "is an operation that relies on an apparatus of assumptions and inclinations, habits and routines, historical associations and cultural practices" (Morgan 2005, 3). It is "the contemplation of images," rather than images themselves, that "exerts the power to arrest the mind" (Morgan 2005, 1). The sense of hearing and tasting can also be understood in this way: these senses too are matters of assumptions, inclinations, and contemplations.

Visualization and auralization in reading

Chu Hsi and Yi Hwang emphasized readings of Confucian classics as the most important form of spiritual practice to attain *li*, principle, and in doing so ultimately to become a sage. They believed the Confucian classics—especially the Four Books and the Five Classics, in which the ancient Confucian sages revealed *li* most clearly—to have transformative power when read repeatedly and deliberately. Readers were supposed to get this power through sensory readings of scriptures, specifically by visualizing and auralizing scriptures.

Chu, who is rated as a great master of Confucianism in Sung Dynasty of China (960-1269) and is thought to have made a synthesis of Neo-Confucianism, firstly emphasized this reading method. Chu pointed out that Confucian sages had people read scriptures in order to edify them (Chu 1977, 121). People reading scriptures were supposed to experience what the sages had experienced. In addition, according to Chu, "if a scholar reads books of sages properly, he can understand what sages meant as if he converses with them face to face" (Chu 1977, 121). Though it was obvious that Confucian readers did not meet the sages directly, they were encouraged to think as if the sages were present at the place they were reading. They had to imagine the sages were talking to them while they were reading. Chu said, "You should always let the words of the sages be in front of your eyes, roll around in your mouth, and circle round in your heart" (Chu 1977, 121). In the process of visualizing sages as if seeing them and of auralizing the sages as if listening to what they said, the senses of vision and hearing should be mobilized.

Yi developed further this brief suggestion of Chu and made it more concrete and sophisticated. Yi was one of the most prominent figures among Korean Confucian scholars. He developed new prospects for Neo-Confucianism philosophy on the basis of his theories of *li* and self-cultivation (Geum 2013, 11). He was also believed to embody the ideal of the virtuous gentleman, the model for Korean Confucian scholars of the scholar who realized the spirit of Neo-Confucianism in his daily life (Geum 2013, 3, 4). However, while Yi is one of the most respected Confucian scholars in Korean history, it was Chu whom Yi admired and regarded as a model Confucian scholar in terms of both scholarship and life. Yi was not the only Korean scholar who tried to retrace the course of Chu's example. Since Neo-Confucianism had been imported from China to Korea, many other Korean Neo-Confucian scholars placed Chu right after the sages in importance and respected him as the authentic successor of Confucius. For instance, An Hyang (1243–1306), a renowned Confucian scholar of the Goryeo Dynasty (918–1392) who first introduced Neo-Confucianism to Korea, regarded the works of Chu as representing the true tradition of Confucius and Mencius. He even said, "Chu Hsi's merits equal those of Confucius. If one wants to study Confucius, one ought to study Chu Hsi first" (Deuchler 1992, 17). Just like An, Yi also accepted Chu as the standard of Confucian scholarship, thinking of him as a kind of semi-sage. While Chu had argued that the *Four Books* should be learned first before reading the *Five Classics* of original Confucianism, Yi asserted that Confucian scholars should understand Confucian scriptures through studying the *Collected Works of Master Chu*, which he regarded as the most important book for Confucian scholars (Geum 2013, 124).

Following Chu's teaching, Yi emphasized that scholars must maintain their minds in the state of *ching* (敬), alertness or mindfulness, all day long. Most importantly, according to Yi, if scholars remain alert and mindful when they read scriptures, they can see images of the sages appear in front of the readers and hear their voices. In "Diagram of the Admonition on Rising Early and Retiring Late," the tenth diagram of Yi's *The Ten Diagrams on Sage Learning*,[3] Yi quoted Chen Po's suggestion that scholars should see the sages and the wise men face to face when reading.

> At this time open your books and see the sage and the wise men face to face. Confucius is seated, Yen Hui and Tseng Tzu are at the front and the rear. Personally, sincerely, and attentively listen to the words of the sacred teacher.

---

3. *The Ten Diagram on Sage Learning* is said to be Yi's masterpiece in which Yi summarized his scholarship of lifetime into ten diagrams and his comments (Geum 2001, iii). In the tenth diagram, "Diagram of the Admonition on Rising Early and Retiring Late," Yi quoted the admonition that had been composed by Chen Po, a Chinese scholar of Sung dynasty, and explained and reinterpreted the admonition in a diagram with his comments. (Kalton 1988, 250; Jeong 2007, 163–164).

Repeatedly referring to the questions and discussions of the disciples, follow them. (Yi 2009, 139)

Scholars would see Confucius, the main character and speaker of scripture, sit before them and his disciples, supporting characters and speakers of scripture, sit around them. According to this diagram, reading in the state of mindfulness was quite the same thing as listening earnestly to the words of the sacred teacher (聖師).

For this experience, scripture should be read aloud and, of course, in a state of mindfulness. Scripture study in Confucianism has been based on reading texts aloud. Chu often said that reading aloud or reciting is the proper way to read scriptures (Gardner 2004, 118), and Yi emphasized that the texts' meaning would become clear by itself if scholars would read them aloud repeatedly sitting in an appropriate position (Geum 2001, 268). Gardner implies this when he observes that this reading is "capable of drawing the reader into a communication with the sages and worthies of antiquity" (Gardner 2004, 112). When Confucian scholars made a voice in reading aloud, they thought they heard the voice of the sage rather than their own voice because the sage was the speaker in the text. They also could visualize the image of the sage who was speaking to them right at the place of reading. In this sense, Neo-Confucian book reading, which was usually reading aloud in the state of mindfulness, was a kind of spiritual practice in which readers used their senses.

Because Yi and other Korean Neo-Confucian scholars thought of Chu almost like a sage, it was natural that Yi tried to see Chu and hear his words in reading *Collected Works of Master Chu*, just as he tried to see and hear Confucius and other sages when he read scriptures of original Confucianism. In *Yeonboboyu*, Yi described his attitude when reading *Collected Works*:

> I tried to get genuine knowledge and to achieve complete understanding [of the text] by kneeling down all day long and fully concentrating my mind. My reading was not different from seeing Chu face to face and learning from him directly because I was highly delighted and had devout faith. Therefore, my view became clearer and more precise day by day and my cultivation grew purer and more solid every day. (Requoted from Geum 2012, 47)

By trying to see Chu face to face and learn from him directly, Yi inherited Chu's suggestion that readers should read scriptures as if they converse with them face to face.

Yi emphasized the importance of the letters of Chu among his many other writings, because they made it easier to visualize and auralize Chu as the author and speaker of the text. Yi compiled fourteen volumes of Chu's letters by selecting letters that he regarded as essential for scholars' study and lives from the forty-eight volumes of Chu's letters. In the foreword, he asserted, "[Chu's letters] teach not only his contemporary disciples but also those who hear his teachings a hundred years later, talking face to face and pulling them by the ears [having them listen carefully]" (Geum 2012, 158). Though Yi knew that some of Chu's letters that he selected were quite private and not directly related to academic discussions, he thought that those letters were particularly helpful. When several disciples of Yi asked why he included those private letters in the compilation, he replied, "I inserted leisurely chats on purpose because I expected readers to experience, by savoring the texts, as if they heard Chu's voices while freely visiting him in person and talking with him" (Geum 2012, 159). According to Yi, Chu's letters that included not only academic discussion but also private conversations were very efficient at setting the scene for visualizing and hearing the semi-sage. Though Chu's private letters did not directly concern deep scholarship, they still helped readers see the great teacher and hear his words. Therefore, to Yi and many other Korean Neo-Confucians, the letters amounted to scriptures.

Reading as tasting: Appreciating the true flavor of books

In addition to visual and aural senses, Chu and Yi developed and recommended a reading method that involved another sense. Both of them employed vivid gustatory imagery for tasting the true flavor of the scriptures. If a sense is a matter of assumptions and inclinations, and concentrating on a sensory image can fill the mind, as suggested above, it can be said that Chu and Yi were encouraging scholars to have gustatory sensations flood their mind. Just as readers could communicate with the sages by reading aloud in mindful state, they also could enjoy the taste of the text by employing the same reading method. According to Gardner, "Savoring the flavor fully, the reader will come to appreciate the true taste. Such imagery is especially apt in a culture of reading where the text normally is recited aloud, by the lips and the mouth" (Gardner 2004, 112). In reciting the text aloud "by the lips and the mouth," they thought that they were chewing "nourishment and spiritual sustenance" (Gardner 2004, 112) provided by the sages and finally tasting it.

Chu argued that Confucian readers should make the text their own and that they had to "experience the text personally" (Gardner 2004, 111). And that personal experience of scripture, according to Chu, was likely to lead to savoring its flavor fully and appreciating its true taste. In *Classified Conversations of Master Chu*, many passages compare reading to tasting. The

Chinese word 味, which corresponds to the English word "taste," can also be translated by "appreciating" and "understanding," just as the English word carries the same range of meanings. Chu used this word frequently in connection with the practice of reading. Chu asserted that if scholars concentrated on reading they could taste the text and that if they penetrated deeply into it they could savor its authentic rich flavor (Chu 1977, 122). Chu also likened meticulous and thorough reading to savoring food. Reading the text with appreciation was compared to chewing well and savoring the flavor (Chu 1977, 131). Scholars should completely understand each passage one at a time and then repeat the whole chapter pondering its meaning, as if they chewed and then felt its taste (Chu 1977, 138, 139). If they read the text thoroughly again and again, they will naturally recognize what they could not previously understand and they will experience a flavor richer than what they had previously known. Scholars cannot experience this subtle flavor unless they are very experienced in reading (Chu 1977, 126). Once the flavor of the text is experienced, they will "recognize its meaning that naturally comes out of the text" (Chu 1977, 128). This thorough and meticulous reading would lead to recognizing *li*, truth or principle, as well as understanding the text fully.

> Generally speaking, one should read thoroughly and minutely, thinking meanings of the text. Reading like this, one's understanding of the text by itself becomes more exact and profound. After one's reading becomes exact and profound, one can naturally recognize principle (*li*). It is just like eating [喫] a fruit. If one bites [咬] the fruit roughly at first, one swallows without knowing its rich taste. But if one chews [嚼] and breaks it into small pieces, its taste naturally comes forth and one gets to know if the fruit is mellow [甛], bitter [苦], sweet [甘], or hot [辛]. At last one can be said to know the taste [味]. (Chu 1977, 124)

In this passage, Chu uses four verbs and four adjectives in order to explain his reading method by employing the metaphor of eating and tasting. While reading itself is compared to eating, reading without understanding the text fully is just biting.[4] Careful and meticulous reading includes two processes of chewing and tasting. He described the experience of tasting vividly, suggesting that there are four distinct flavors: mellow, bitter, sweet, and hot. The readers who follow his reading method can understand exactly and profoundly the text and finally recognize principle, as if they not only eat food but also appreciate its various tastes.

---

4. Chu often compared reading to eating food in *Classified Conversations of Master Chu*. For example, he likened reading to drinking wine and to taking medicine. According to Chu, scholars who like reading would keep reading, as if a person who likes drinking would not stop after drinking just one glass of wine but would like to drink another. Likewise, one should keep reading as if medicine should be taken many times to exert a remedial effect. (Chu 1977, 128)

Yi also likened reading to eating and tasting, describing them as if scriptures themselves were food and the object of the gustatory sense. He argued that scholars should enjoy the happiness of knowing "the taste of reading" (Geum 2001, 42). As mentioned above, Yi asserted that scholars should begin studying by reading *Collected Works of Master Chu* and acquaint themselves with them. If they then read the Four Books after having read *Collected Works*, Yi says, then "every word of the sages will be tasty" (Geum 2013, 124).

He described his own reading as eating scriptures. In a poem he wrote when he was fifty-nine years old, he contrasts his own eating of the book with that of a bookworm that was eating the book without knowing its taste.

> Being a gray-haired old man who is gravely ill and incapable
> I have been eating into the book, making a pair with a bookworm
> How can it know the taste though it eats the letters?
> Heaven grants me many books in which I find my pleasure.
> (Requoted from Geum 2013, 50)

In this poem, Yi's reading is described as eating the book while knowing its taste. Though a bookworm also eats the book physically, this eating cannot rival his own because the bookworm does not know the full flavor. In another poem that he composed when he was sixty-one years old, he wrote, "true taste is in the text / my satisfaction from it is much bigger than that from all kinds of delicacies" (Geum 2013, 51). Yi equates Confucian scholars' reading of scriptures to eating the text and savoring its taste.

These two Neo-Confucian masters did not describe the gustatory experience of reading simply for poetic effect. For them, tasting the scriptures was a real experience. As I explained above, Chu emphasized that the personal experience of the text that will result in appreciating its true taste. Similarly, Yi argues that the flavor of the text "cannot be expressed in language." He continues:

> Scholars themselves should try to get at the explanation by tasting its deep flavor and having real experience of it. ⋯ [Asking about the taste of the text] is just like asking other persons how the food they are eating tastes. One can know the taste of the food only after eating what other persons are eating and after tasting what they are tasting. Is it right if one asks other persons how it tastes without eating it oneself at all? Scholars must never fail to experience fully the taste [of the text] first-hand. (Yi 2010, 152)

Experiencing the taste of reading was not just a metaphoric expression. Though Yi mentioned it for the purpose of introducing it to scholars and encouraging them to experience it, Yi thought that it was beyond description. Chu and Yi advised Neo-Confucian scholars to gain direct sensory experience of tasting scriptures.

Chu and Yi likened reading scriptures to eating them and understanding them fully to savoring its true flavor. They not only appropriated metaphors of eating and tasting but also created the gustatory imagery for the taste of books while reading them. To them, reading was a complicated process that involved biting, chewing, eating, and tasting the words of the sages.

Conclusion

Chu and Yi encouraged the Confucian scholar to activate at least three senses when reading a text, over and above the experience of merely reading the characters of the text. First, the text should be recited aloud so the reciters would hear their own voices, sometimes along with those of their colleagues. They imagined, furthermore, that the voices they were hearing while reading were those of the ancient sages themselves and of their disciples, namely "the wise men." Secondly, while hearing the voices of the sages, the reciting scholars would visualize their images, seeking personal communion with them. Finally, the meditative reading of scholars was frequently likened to savoring a text's flavor, with the act of reading being described as eating, biting, chewing, and tasting. When the readers recited the text aloud, pronouncing each syllable using their tongues, lips and mouths, they engaged in a gustatory experience: "chewing" and "tasting" the ancient classics.

While I limited myself to the sensory aspects of only Chu and Yi's reading methods, research on the sensory readings of Neo-Confucian scholars should be expanded further. As the influence of Chu and Yi on Confucian scholars was significant, there will be many examples of other Chinese and Korean scholars' sensory reading. Because a sense is "an operation that relies on an apparatus of assumptions and inclinations" and because "the contemplation of images" has "the power to arrest the mind" (Morgan 2005, 1, 3), it is clear that the senses were deeply involved in these scholars' communion with the sages through reading though they did not physically see the sages, hear their words, or actually consume their books. Their religious experience began from reading scriptures by using their senses and aimed at a sensory experience.

5

PERFORMING SCRIPTURES: RITUALIZING SACRED TEXTS IN KOREAN SHAMANIC RECITATION OF SCRIPTURES

Concerning shamans and shamanic texts

I would like to clarify some English terms that I chose to translate Korean words in this chapter before I begin to discuss *seolwi-seolgyeong*. First, it was not without reservations that I chose the word "shaman." I am aware that "shaman" is a highly controversial word because of the variety of people this term encompasses. I decided to use it in this chapter to translate the Korean terms *musogin* [무속인] and *mudang* [무당], after concluding that it is an easy and passable word for English-speaking readers. The first word that most Korean-English dictionaries suggest for the translation of these two terms is "shaman." For me, "shamanism" designates a religious entity that involves a community led by a shaman (or shamans) who provides a worldview and practices for the community members. I confess that I was confused in choosing between the adjectives "shamanic" or "shamanistic." I preferred to use "shamanistic" because I thought it covers broader meanings that are related to shamanism. So, I used "shamanistic" for the title of the original version of this chapter, which was "Performing Scriptures: Ritualizing Written Texts in *Seolwi-seolgyeong*, the Korean Shamanistic Recitation of Scriptures." However, I changed "shamanistic" to "shamanic" in this chapter. I decided to use "shamanic" to describe the activities, utterances, and thoughts that shamans have or make in person, whereas I use "shamanistic" to designate practices and beliefs that lay members of the community share with their shaman.

Additionally, the word "written" in the original title was removed, changing "Ritualizing Written Texts in *Seolwi-seolgyeong*" to "Ritualizing Sacred Texts in *Seolwi-seolgyeong*." When I worked on the original article to make it proper for this book, it occurred to me that shamans (*gyeonggaek*; see below) of the Chungcheong provinces have learned and inherited sacred texts orally from their teachers without receiving books. It is true that most of the sacred texts they are using existed in book form, some of which were Daoist scriptures as will be shown. However, Chungcheong shamans have learned and used their texts orally for generations. It should be noted that they have developed ways of materializing and embodying oral texts, which will be demonstrated in this chapter. By writing the names of gods who are the main characters of scriptures, by making paper figures of them, and by shaping the weapons described in scriptures as symbolic forms, the semantic dimension of scriptures is embodied to ritualize their iconic dimension. In that these embodied figures and papers are used in ritual performances, here we are witnessing how the performative dimension of scriptures is ritualized also. More attention should be paid to this phenomenon because it suggests an example of materializing, or "iconizing," oral sacred texts.

Though some sacred texts used by shamans in the Chungcheong area originally came from Daoist scriptures that surely existed as codex or woodblock printed books, the materialization of oral texts does not seem to be influenced by the book form of the original texts. That observation can also be made of the sacred texts of Jeju shamans. In Jeju Island, Korea, shamans have learned and used oral texts only, without any written texts. Jeju shamans represent some contents of their oral texts, which often outline the genealogies of gods and explain the origins of rituals, by making paper figures which they use in rituals. Therefore, the embodiment and materialization of the contents of oral texts should be investigated by further research.

Performing scriptures by reciting, writing and materializing

seolwi-seolgyeong is a shamanic ritual that has been handed down around North and South Chungcheong Provinces, South Korea. *Seolwi-seolgyeong* has characteristics that distinguish it from other Korean shamanic rituals. Above all, the main part of the whole ritual consists of the recitation of scriptures, in which shamans invoke the power of the gods appearing in scriptures. Shamans of Chungcheong area are commonly called "*gyeongjaengi*" or "*gyeonggaek*," which means "a person who deals with scriptures," and their activity in rituals is called "*dokgyeong*," which literally means "reading scriptures." From these names that emphasize scriptures, we can see that the recitation of scriptures has been recognized as the most important part of this ritual. While shamans in most other areas of Korea perform their rituals standing and enacting the stories of gods, the *gyeonggaek*s in the relatively long *seolwi-seolgyeong* rituals of the Chungcheong area remain seated and recite scriptures while beating a drum (*buk* or a double-headed drum called *janggu*) and a gong (*jing*). In addition, unlike shamans of most other areas in Korea, the shamans in the *seolwi-seolgyeong* ritual do not serve the gods lavish meals. Instead, the recitation itself is the main offering, and this is how one pleases the gods, though sometimes a very simple meal is also offered. *Gyeonggaek*s also strongly rebuke and subdue evil spirits through the power of scriptures, while in most other shamanic rituals evil spirits are either propitiated or not directly dealt with at all. The *seolwi-seolgyeong* ritual is distinctive in that the *gyeonggaek* shaman is able to wield tremendous power in invoking gods and subduing evil spirits without ever having to leave his or her seat.

In this chapter, I demonstrate how the sacred power of scriptures is maximized and how their sacred status is secured in *seolwi-seolgyeong* by articulating a comprehensive way of performing scriptures. Above all, in *seolwi-seolgyeong*, the gods' presence is made possible by performing scriptures in several ways: scriptures are recited, written, and materialized. Just like in Jewish, Christian, and Islamic traditions (Peters 2007, 140), scriptures are recited and what is recited is accepted as the divine beings' own words in *seolwi-seolgyeong*. It is clear that the sacred power of scriptures is mobilized primarily by being recited. But writing and materializing scriptures are also involved. "Seolwi," the first half of the name of this ritual, is commonly understood as making or installing various geometric paper figures and banners that represent or contain the contents of the scriptures. By making *seolwi*, scriptures are materialized and their power is made visible and physically available. Though the scriptures themselves in book form are rarely visible in the ritual place, the sacred status and power of scriptures that suppress the evil spirits are made clearly visible by their materialized contents and the embodiment of their main characters.

Furthermore, in *seolwi-seolgyeong* we can see how various rituals privilege and distinguish scriptures from other things (Bell 1992, 74, 88–93; Watts 2006 [2008]; Watts 2017, 257–260, 266). First, scriptures themselves as well as their words are distinguished from other texts when lay participants as well as shamans agree that scriptures are the words of divine beings. As a result, the performative activity of reciting the scriptures is equated with proclaiming divine words. Ritualized scriptures distinguish themselves as sacred and as able to exercise the power of "realities thought to transcend the powers of human actors" (Bell 1992, 74). The recitation is a ritualized act that is differentiated as important, powerful, and sacred (Bell 1992, 90). The success of *seolwi-seolgyeong* relies heavily on various recitation techniques which are necessary in order to defeat evil spirits and heal patients efficiently. This ritualization is more effective when the recitation is performed more skillfully. Finally, the contents of scriptures are ritualized when shamans materialize them into paper figures on the basis of their interpretation of the cosmology and theology in scriptures. This material ritualization makes the contents seem so sacred that they are able to subdue evil spirits and resolve human problems.

Scriptures used in *Seolwi-seolgyeong* rituals

Though there are different interpretations of the name of this ritual according to local shamans, the first half of the name, *seolwi*, usually designates figures and banners that are used in shamanic rituals in the Chungcheong area or the activity of making and installing these figures and banners, while the second half, *seolgyeong*, is understood as reciting scriptures (Gu 2009, 21). Paper figures reflect the core contents of scriptures and are believed to help defeat evil spirits. Paper banners, on which are written the names of gods appearing in scriptures and sometimes words, phrases, or passages from scriptures, carry out the same function. The second part of the title, "*seolgyeong*," signifies the recitation of scriptures that is performed for the purpose of solving human problems with the aid of the gods (Im 2011, 12–13; Jang 2013, 342). Shamans and participants in the Chungcheong area often refer to the *seolwi-seolgyeong* as an *anjeungut*, the "sitting rite." But strictly speaking, *anjeungut* is a more comprehensive term than *seolwi-seolgyeong* because sometimes it designates simpler rituals in which shamans are seated and recite scriptures without making and installing paper figures or banners. A *gut* is a general term for a Korean traditional shamanic ritual of propitiating the gods, performed by shamans for the benefit of individuals, families, and village communities. The name *anjeungut* underscores the fact that the "sitting" (*anjeun*) dimension of this particular *gut* is what sets it apart from other *guts* (Im 2011, 14).

In *anjeunguts*, shamans generally do not read from texts, but rather recite from memory. By the early twentieth century, the job of reciting scriptures to repel evil spirits was often taken on by blind persons, who naturally could not read books in the literal sense (Gu 2009, 36–37; Yi 1989, 264–265). However, shamans and participants also use the term *dokgyeong*, literally meaning "reading scriptures," to signify the main activities in the ritual. This term emphasizes the literal, textual, bookish dimension of scripture, because the activity of reading requires a book in its physical form. "*Dokgyeong*" can refer to the actual recitation activity within the *gut* but can also simply refer to the whole *anjeungut* (Gu 2009, 178), demonstrating that the recitation of scripture is the basic component of the ritual.

Some scholars think that performers of *anjeungut* should not be included in the category of shamans because they are not possessed by gods during the ritual, unlike shamans in many other areas in Korea. However, the view that *anjeungut* should be regarded as a shamanic ritual is more prevalent. Western and Japanese scholars who visited Korea in the late nineteenth century or early twentieth century considered *anjeungut* a kind of shamanic ritual. More contemporary scholars also include *gyeonggaek*s among shamans who stand between gods and human beings, who try to alleviate human suffering with the help of the gods, and who carry the gods' messages to human beings (Kim, Park, and An 2012, 15; Im 2011, 52; Park 2014, 604). Most of all, *gyeonggaek*s themselves think that they are *musogin*s, Korean shamans. They are active members of the Korean federation of shamans. *Gyeonggaek*s of Chungcheong Provinces whose main ritual job is the seated recitation of scriptures have played the same role as shamans in other areas, that is, as a mediator between the divine realm and the human realm. They play the role of a healer who treats human suffering or a diviner who tells clients' fortune with the aid of the gods or sometimes on the basis of sacred knowledge that is unknown to lay participants (Kim, Park, and An 2012, 29-30). It is true that they are not possessed by gods or spirits during the ritual, but they invite gods to the ritual place and consult them in order to be given divine messages. On the other hand, *gyeonggaek*s were sometimes more respected than other shamans because they were literate and performed rituals while sitting demurely, in contrast to the "primitive" gesticulations associated with most *gut*s. While conservative Confucian scholars of the late Joseon period (seventeenth to nineteenth centuries) abhorred and prohibited *gut*s performed by the shamans possessed by spirits who often danced and hopped during the ritual, they did not ban *anjeungut*s where scriptures are read by persons seated decently (Kim, Park, and An 2012, 16).

*Anjeungut*s can be divided into two types, according to their purposes. The first type, called *antaekgut*, is conducted to invoke the blessings of the guardian gods who govern the different aspects of the home, such as the building, the plot, the main bedroom, the living room, and the kitchen, asking for the peace and stability of the household. Though these favorable gods are offered a simple meal during this ritual, the whole procedure is mainly carried out verbally. For instance, the purification ritual that is performed at the beginning of the *antaekgut* is comprised of recited scriptures, mostly the *Bujeonggyeong* ("Scripture for Impurity") that is recited to remove the impurity of the ritual place, and the *Bosingyeong* ("Scripture of Self-protection") which proclaims that the shaman reciting the scripture is a descendent of the heavenly gods and thus possesses divine mysterious power (An 2009, 106–108; 148–150).[1] The core part of *antaekgut*, calling the gods and communicating with each god, also consists of reciting relevant scriptures.

The second type of *anjeungut* is conducted for the purpose of warding off misfortunes or calamities. *Byeonggut*, "the ritual for sick persons," is the most commonly performed of this second type of *anjeungut* rituals. While the first type of *anjeungut* can be carried out without paper banners and figures, they are usually required for the second type. The main part of the *byeonggut*s is, again, the recitation of scriptures, but in these rites the *gyeonggaek*s also perform dramatic actions. *Gyeonggaek*s recite scriptures to invoke the power of Cheonjon, the highest god of Heaven, to summon warrior gods who help subdue the evil spirits to the ritual place, and to repel the evil spirits that cause illness and other misfortunes (Kim, Park, and An 2012, 35–41). It is the power of scriptures that subdues the evil spirits called *dongto* and *sagwi*, expels them from the home, and cures sick persons. Sometimes scriptures are recited in *byeonggut*s for the purpose of appeasing dead ancestors' deep-rooted rancor and sending them peacefully to the otherworld. *Byeonggut*s are usually conducted for three, five, or seven days depending on the severity of the conditions. The god Seongju, who governs the house building, decides the necessary period of time by means of an oracle. It is said that in particularly severe circumstances, the ritual could take up to one hundred days. Before a *byeonggut* is conducted, an *antaekgut* is performed to purify the house and invite the household gods. During the *byeonggut*, the recitations are punctuated by intermittent dramatic performances, such as dispatching ancestors to the otherworld after quelling their grudges, beckoning the warrior gods to descend from the heavens, and subduing evil spirits by trapping them in a bottle and physically removing them from the house.

The scripture that shamans recite most often for repelling evil spirits is *Okchugyeong*, originally a Daoist scripture. The second most important scripture for the same purpose is *Cheonjipalyanggyeong*, originally an apocryphal Buddhist scripture. But there are much shorter texts in the form of incantations or prayers which are recited in each sequence of *seolwiseolgyeong*. The last text recited in the ritual is *Toesingyeong*, a brief scripture for sending back the gods away from the ritual place. The contents

---

1. Shamans and the house owners are also required to bathe themselves in preparation for the ritual, but their bathing is not a part of *antaekgut*. While *antaekgut* usually begins in the evening and ends at dawn, bathing, along with cleaning the house, is done in the morning on the day the ritual is performed. Purifications conducted as a part of *antaekgut* consists just of reciting scriptures (Kim, Park and An 2012, 79).

of many texts used in *seolwi-seolgyeong* threaten evil spirits. Though some are crude incantations, most of them are scriptures that have their own logic derived from other religious traditions, such as the Confucian theory of five elements or Buddhist cosmology (Kim, Park and An 2012, 46–47). The contents of threats against evil spirits that are contained in scriptures are "not simple intimidation but are explained by cause-and-effect relationships and secure their legitimacy firmly by citing from Confucian, Buddhist, and Daoist thought" (An 2010a, 146). By reciting these scriptures, shamans therefore invoke deities not only traditional to Korean shamanism, but also those who originated in Daoism and Buddhism, and they subdue evil spirits by their power (Im 2011, 17).

However, obvious threats do not appear at all in the two most important scriptures for removing evil spirits and misfortunes, *Okchugyeong* and *Cheonjipalyangsinjugyeong*. These two scriptures are mainly composed of teachings given to human beings by transcendental beings, Cheongjon and the Buddha. Originally, the revealer and the speaker of *Okchugyeong*, the Gucheon-eungwon-noeseong-bohwa-cheonjon, "the heavenly god of universal transformation of the sound of the thunder of responding origin in the nine heavens," was one of the three major deities of the Shenxiao Daoist tradition in China. He represents life and the esoteric practice of thunder, and shows the explicit influence of Buddhism (*vajra*) (Schipper and Verellen 2004, 1082–1083). Shamans pray to this heavenly god for resolving troubles in human lives. He is believed to save human beings by revealing his true way. This Daoist scripture is thought to have been adopted by Korean shamans because of its postscript, which states: "if you recite this scripture, you can annihilate all evil spirits and overcome all kinds of illness" (An 2009, 97).[2] This is the most powerful scripture that

---

2. *Okchugyeong* or *Okchubogyeong* (*Yushubaojing* 玉樞寶經 in Chinese) is the most important scripture in Korean shamanism. It consists of 6 divine incantations (or prayers), 9 chapters on heaven, 11 chapters on earth, 15 chapters on humans, and 15 talismans (Gu 2009, 253). It was originally a scripture of the early Shenxiao (神霄) tradition, one of the Chinese Daoist schools in Southern Song period (1127–1279). This book is regarded as a work of the early thirteenth century but the earliest extant version has a colophon dated 1333. Since *Okchugyeong* is mentioned in *Suhoji*, a very popular Chinese novel written in the fourteenth century, this scripture seems to have circulated in China in this period at the latest (An 2009, 92). This book is included in the Fourth Daozang (Daoist Canon) which was collected mainly in 1444 during the Ming dynasty. Its original full name, *Jiutianyingyuanleishengpuhuatianzunyushubaojing* is translated into English as "Precious Book of the Jade Pivot, Spoken by the Heavenly Worthy (God) of Universal Transformation of the Sound of the Thunder of Responding Origin in the Nine Heavens." Concerning the Shenxiao tradition and this scripture, see Schipper and Verellen 2004, 1081–1095.

Okchugyeong seems to have come into Korea in the fourteenth century at the latest, since *Gyeonggukdaejeon*, the royal law book of the Joseon dynasty (1392–1910) that was

can "melt down" evil spirits (or their bones) by being recited (Gu 2009, 44). In *anjeunguts*, shamans repeatedly recite parts of *Okchugyeong* that they think are appropriate for their clients' situation. *Cheonjipalyangsinjugyeong* begins with the words "thus I have heard," just as in other Buddhist sutras, and it takes the form of the Buddha's teaching, but reflects a Daoist understanding of the cosmos and human beings. There are no direct threats against evil spirits in these two scriptures. They are about understanding the world and the ideal lives of human beings, as explained by Cheonjon and the Buddha (An 2010b, 16, 21).

It is fairly understandable that people think evil spirits can be subdued by the recitation of the scriptures in which divine beings rebuke and threaten them. Scriptures can be "the most important symbol of power" through which gods talk and act (Wimbush 2012, 163). As shown above, however, a scripture can subdue evil spirits even if it does not speak against evil spirits directly, because of the divine authority and power that is present in it. Scriptures can "convey mysterious power that has its origin in another realm—from God—and that can be employed to influence others" (Wimbush 2012, 177). This is the power of the sacred scripture. Reciters and hearers, as well as readers, think that "scriptures are relevant, cryptic, and perfect because they think scriptures come from God [gods]" (Watts 2017, 256 citing Kugel 1997, 14–23). In the ritual space of *seolwi-seolgyeong*, hearers of recited scriptures, as well as the reciters themselves, believe that the scriptures come from the gods. Because participants think scriptures come from gods, they assume that scriptures not only contain divine messages but also divine power. Though human hearers may not understand the meaning of a scripture being recited, its power can be utilized as long as people believe it to be of divine origin. Thanks to the ritualization of this belief through recitation and materialization, scriptures are recognized as sacred beings. Shamans who have special knowledge of scriptures exert divine authority and the power of scriptures by reciting them.

In *seolwi-seolgyeong*, we find the belief expressed that scriptures recited by shamans can mobilize the gods appearing in the scriptures, subdue evil spirits, and solve human problems. The power of scriptures enables shamans to threaten and defeat evil spirits, rather than merely propitiate them. It is certain that reciting, or literally "reading," scriptures is at

---

compiled during the mid-fifteenth century, attests that this scripture was recited by Daoist priests. Though in the early Joseon period, Daoist rituals were performed by Daoists who held government office, Daoism was considered heretical by Confucian scholars and Daoist offices were closed from the sixteenth century on. This Daoist scripture was accepted by Korean shamans, however, and became the most important shamanic scripture. See An 2009, 96–98; Gu 2009, 96; Jang 2013, 354–356.

Figure 5.1. *Seolwi*, making or installing paper figures and banners. Photo: author.

Figure 5.2. A *gyeonggaek* reciting scriptures while remaining seated in a local festival. Photo: author.

the center of this ritual. However, *seolwi-seolgyeong* has also devised other means of maximizing the power of scriptures through the visualization and materialization of scriptures.

Maximizing sacred status and power of scripture by recitation and materialization

Many Korean Buddhists have claimed the power of scriptures by reciting and copying them (see Yoo 2010 [2012]). However, it is rare among Korean religious traditions for scriptures to be recited, written, and materialized within the space of a single ritual. Because *seolwi-seolgyeong* involves reciting, writing, and materializing scriptures, it can be said that *seolwi-seolgyeong* is a comprehensive example of the performance of scriptures. Though nowadays there are fewer and fewer shamans who are well acquainted with the contents of the scriptures, traditionally it was necessary for shamans in the Chungcheong Provinces to be versed in the contents in order to be qualified to perform *seolwi-seolgyeong*.[3] Even if the performers and the audience in the ritual arena may not understand the recitation, the evil spirits do, and they are influenced by it. *Gyeonggaek*s should also be skilled in the recitation techniques that are required for inviting gods and subduing evil spirits efficiently in various situations.

---

3. It is necessary to master shamanic scriptures in order to become a *gyeonggaek*. Applicants master scriptures by learning from established *gyeonggaek*s both orally and in writing. In the past, when blind persons often played the role of *gyeonggaek*s, they had to learn everything orally but nowadays there are few blind persons who take the job. Applicants listen and learn by heart what their teachers recite, then they write it in notebooks and memorize it (Park 2010, 68). Some applicants receive the manuscripts that their teachers wrote and recopy them in order to memorize them (An 2010a, 150). Those who have little acquaintance with classical Chinese cannot learn scriptures written in classical Chinese characters with Korean endings, but can only listen to what is recited and write its phonetic pronunciation in Korean (Oh 1997, 98). Recently two noticeable changes among *gyeonggaek*s and the scriptures they are using have been observed. First, the number of experts in shamanic scriptures is decreasing drastically. A survey conducted in 1976 showed that there were two thousand and fourteen *gyeonggaek*s practicing in North Chungcheong Province, while the number of other types of shamans in that area was only sixteen (Seo 1991). But nowadays this proportion has reversed in Chungcheong Provinces, perhaps because the shamans who perform *guts* more dynamically are more popular. Second, the proportion of the shamans who do not understand the contents of scriptures in classical Chinese rises year by year. This change is predictable, as the study of Chinese characters has declined drastically since the modernization of Korea beginning in the late nineteenth century. As these shamans recite scriptures in classical Chinese without knowing their meaning just like uttering incantations, more changes in the text of scriptures come about (An 2010b, 9). Though it is true that changes and the creation of new scriptures have always taken place because the efficacy of the ritual recitation is regarded more highly than its accuracy, those who know only the phonetic values of the text venture to change scriptures more quickly on the basis of their own suppositions about the contents of scriptures (Gu 2009, 137).

Performing Scriptures

In addition, they should be expert in making paper banners and figures, that is, in materializing scriptures. In *seolwi-seolgyeong*, scriptures are materialized in order to threaten, trap, and expel evil spirits by making and displaying the banners on which are written the names of the gods in the scriptures or important scriptural passages and figures that reflect the contents of scriptures.

Shamans and the laity in the Chungcheong region say that the most important skill in the performance of *anjeungut*s is recitation technique, the second is playing the drum and gong, and the third is knowledge of the texts. The recitation techniques are considered most important in the first place because they have a decisive effect on the outcome of the ritual. In *seolwi-seolgyeong*, various reciting techniques and methods should be utilized according to the purpose of the ritual and the condition of the patient. The recitation techniques making use of rhythm, tone, pitch, tempo, and dynamics are all crucial for pleasing gods and threatening evil spirits. *Gyeonggaek*s are aware that the better their recitation techniques, the more efficacious the ritual (Han 2017). For instance, in the invocation of the warrior gods and the subduing of the evil spirits, reciters must use urgent and commanding tones with a quick tempo and beat the drums and gongs intensely in order to achieve the goal. They cannot successfully placate the deep-rooted rancor of the ancestors unless they recite the relevant scripture in an appropriately plaintive voice.

Recitation techniques are also counted as most important among the three skills of *gyeonggaek*s because the divine beings are believed to come to the ritual place and work there only through skillful recitations. Many religious traditions in which scriptures are recited tend "to use tone and rhythm to project the voice and make the reading more memorable" (Watts 2017, 259). But tone and rhythm are important here not only for hearing and memorizing scriptures but also for fulfilling the purpose of the ritual and for having the divine be involved in the ritual. In *seolwi-seolgyeong*, these techniques are necessary in order for the gods to become the subjects and agents of the ritual. As Kimberley Patton properly points out, we often forget that the divine is not just the object but "the subject and agent of the religious action" (Patton 2009, 15). The gods who listen to the skillful recitation are persuaded to come to the ritual place and do their work as the main characters of the ritual; they give orders to *gyeonggaek*s, overpower the evil spirits, heal patients, and give notice if the ritual was successful or not. The recitation, the activity of performing scriptures, is distinguished as more important and powerful than other ritual acts when people equate it with proclaiming the divine words. But this ritualization of the recitation must be completed and consolidated by proper techniques. Without them, the divine words are not efficacious and the sacred power of scriptures is not revealed.

Some scholars do not agree with the view that recitation techniques are the most important among the three skills. They argue that the importance of recitation techniques is overemphasized due to the fact that lay participants do not understand what is recited (An 2010a, 150; Kim, Park and An 2012, 48–49; Oh 1997, 100–101). These scholars emphasize the contents of scriptures rather than the technique for reciting them, asserting that knowledge of the texts should be counted as the most important skill. It is understandable that the host, the owner of the house where the ritual is performed, and other participants who have not had professional training cannot understand recited scriptures, which are mainly composed of Classical Chinese words with Korean endings. It is true that some *gyeonggaek*s are proud of their specialized knowledge of the texts and their ability to choose and recite specific texts depending on the situation. However, it should be noted that shamans' competence with scriptures matters mainly because it is an efficient tool for inviting the gods and defeating evil spirits, not because the knowledge itself has more value than recitation techniques. Gods and evil spirits are thought to understand the meaning of what is recited and respond to it. The contents of scriptures are privileged, not because they are learned and studied by human beings but because they are efficacious in expelling evil spirits and healing patients.

The conduct of *seolwi-seolgyeong* employs not only the sound of reciting scriptures but also the visualization and materialization of scriptures to call the gods and subdue evil spirits. Traditionally, *gyeonggaek*s are trained to be skillful in making *seolwi*s, paper banners and figures in *changhoji*, traditional Korean paper made from mulberry bark (Oh 1997, 113). They write on it the names of gods or phrases from scriptures and they carve into it images of gods or symbolic traps reflecting the contents of scriptures. These banners and figures therefore show the words of the gods and their majestic world to evil spirits. A *byeonggut*, which is the most common ritual among the second type of *anjeungut*s and is performed to heal sick persons, begins by writing the names of gods or words of scriptures and making paper figures. Scriptures are materialized through these banners and figures, which are important material ingredients in a successful performance of *seolwi-seolgyeong*.

Many *gyeonggaek*s say that they make paper figures on the basis of their understanding of the contents of *Okchugyeong* (Im 2009, 83, 90–91). In this sense, the process of creating them can be said to be interpreting the scripture.[4] When they make these figures, they embody and visualize the divine wisdom and the cosmology shown in scriptures, especially that of *Okchugyeong*, as they understand it (Im 2009, 93). *Gyeonggaek*s represent their interpretation of scriptures as paper figures. In other words, the semantic dimension of scriptures is ritualized iconically in the creation of *seolwi*s.

Paper banners, on which the names of gods and important passages from *Okchugyeong* or other scriptures are written, extend the recitation visually (Im 2009, 95). Paper figures, which are materialized scriptures, have the power of trapping evil spirits in them as well as scaring them away (Park 2010, 74). They enable the power of scriptures to be exerted in full measure. Im explains how recited scriptures, written scriptures, and materialized scriptures work together, in the following way:

> In hearing the scripture for expelling evil, the evil spirit begins to be frightened. And its fear doubles when it sees the banners of the words from scriptures, which are installed in the hall in which the ritual is conducted. Eventually, it is trapped in the *jinbeop* [battle array] of the paper figures. Now it can be put in a bottle by the *beopsa* [*gyeonggaek*].[5] The voice of the *beopsa* reciting scriptures makes a sound effect that threatens the evil spirit and the *seolwi* produces a visual one. The patient and his or her family who watch the ritual become convinced that the evil spirit will soon be controlled. Basically, therefore, the *seolwi* that is installed in the ritual place works together with the content of scriptures that is recited by the *beopsa*. (Im 2011, 22)

Evil spirits understand what is recited, written, or materialized and are overwhelmed by its power. They are frightened and subdued when they hear the recitation of scriptures and see words from scriptures and materialized forms of scriptures.

To utilize the power of scriptures to the utmost, shamans should recite scriptures by using various techniques, write the names of gods that appear in scriptures or important passages from scriptures on paper banners, and materialize scriptures by making figures that reflect their contents.

---

4. Though these *gyeonggaek*s argue that their paper figures come from the scripture, it should be noted that most paper figures of the Chungcheong region are not much different from those of other areas in Korea where shamans do not claim scriptures as the basis of paper figures. It is possible that *gyeonggaek*s, at least sometimes, ascribe meanings extracted from the scripture to the preexisting paper figures rather than creating the figures on the basis of the scripture.

5. "*Beopsa*" originally means a Buddhist monk who is an expert and teacher of dharma. But the meaning of this term has been extended to designate a male shaman, or more specifically in Chungcheong Provinces a *gyeonggaek*. It is thought that Korean shamanism accepted this term to show more respect for shamans by equating them with respectable Buddhist monks (Oh 2016).

Figure 5.3. *Seolwis* reflecting the contents of scriptures. Photo: author.

Figure 5.4. *Seolwis* reflecting the contents of scriptures. Photo: author.

Conclusion

In the *seolwi-seolgyeong* ritual, scriptures are considered so powerful that they can take over the other dynamics of shamanic rituals, such as possession or dance. In this ritual, scriptures are performed mainly by recitation. But the recitation is supplemented with other ways of performing scriptures, namely writing and materializing them in paper, to maximize their power. When scriptures are written and materialized to be used as the shaman's tool, as well as recited in the ritual, their contents are realized and simultaneously their sacred status is established. Recitation of scriptures is the nucleus of *seolwi-seolgyeong*. Properly performed recitations are believed to invite the gods to the ritual place and enable them to work there, as well as to subdue evil spirits. During most of the ritual, shamans are seated and recite scriptures to pray for peace in the household and expel evil spirits from it. Though lay participants do not understand the meaning of recited scriptures, it is still regarded as important because gods and evil spirits understand it. There are scriptures whose contents are related to threatening or defeating evil spirits. But the most powerful scriptures that can even melt down the bones of evil spirits are those that focus on the teachings of the heavenly god and the Buddha concerning the cosmos and the human beings. For *seolwi-seolgyeong* to be most efficacious, recitation of scriptures should be supported by materializing and visualizing scriptures. Evil spirits become frightened and weakened when they see and read paper banners on which the names of gods appearing in scriptures and passages from them are written. The paper figures that visualize gods scare evil spirits and those that reflect the cosmology and theology of scriptures can hedge them in and trap them.

In this ritual process, scriptures are privileged and distinguished as sacred beings in several ways.[6] First, scriptures are distinguished as sacred beings when shamans and other participants in *seolwi-seolgyeong* agree that the words in them are no less than the words of divine beings. Scriptures ritualized as such can exert transcendental power. Second, the ritual activity of performing scriptures, the recitation, is believed to be the proclamation of the divine words. This ritualization should be completed and consolidated by proper techniques, without which the divine words cannot be efficacious. Third, the contents of scriptures are also ritualized when the teachings of the divine beings in the scriptures are considered so sacred that the contents can defeat evil spirits and heal the patients and when shamans materialize them as paper figures on the basis of their interpretation of the cosmology and theology in scriptures.

---

6. For more about scriptures as sacred beings, see the other essays in Watts and Yoo (2021).

6

POWERFUL TINY SCRIPTURES:
MINIATURE SUTRAS IN KOREAN BUDDHISM

Miniature sutras in Korea

Korean lay Buddhists, most of whom are unable to recite or read scriptures that are mainly written in classical Chinese, have approached and used Buddhist scriptures in non-semantic ways. They have developed various ways of repeating and possessing scriptures in order to use as well as possible the power and status of those sacred texts (see Chapter 2). According to the pioneering study of James Watts (2006 [2008]), scripture can be ritualized along three dimensions: the semantic, the iconic, and the performative. In the possession of scriptures and various ways of repeating them, such as reciting and copying scriptures, turning rotating sutra cases, or playing sutra CDs, it is the iconic and performative dimensions of scriptures, rather than the semantic, that are conspicuously revealed. In this chapter, I turn to another way in which contemporary Korean lay Buddhists mobilize the sacred status and power of scriptures in the iconic dimension by how they create and utilize miniature sutras.

Miniature sutras, and Buddhist scriptures in general, have iconic status and sacred power that are quite autonomous from the semantic dimension of scriptures. This autonomy differs from the influence that any text comes to possess in the process of its interpretation. Paul Ricoeur has shown that a written text can separate itself from its original semantic context, such as its author, its initial audience, and situation, and acquire a status independent of them. When what is spoken is written and becomes a text, it assumes an object-like character and is "decontextualized" from its original setting and becomes open to innumerable "recontextualizations" (Ricoeur 1995, 219). In this way, the text obtains autonomy and moreover "iconicity" (Ricoeur 1976, 42). According to Ricoeur, iconicity is not separate from the semantic dimension of the text, in that this iconicity is secured when the text breaks away from its original understanding and is interpreted in different situations and new ways. Yet Buddhist scriptures often possess an iconicity that is separate from their semantic contexts. The recontextualization of Buddhist scriptures comes about as a result of their own sacred status. Scriptures that are regarded as sacred beings perform supernatural work, which Buddhists expect to be carried out independent of their content, not only in ritual situations but also in daily life. Miniature sutras of contemporary Korean Buddhism are so small that they are very difficult to read without a magnifying glass. Indeed, few lay Buddhists who possess and carry these miniature sutras even try to understand their content. Instead, they expect the miniature sutras to transform the Buddha statues in their home into the real and living Buddha, thereby bringing blessings and benefits to their lives.

It should also be noted that the scriptures' iconic status as "the word-body of the Buddha" (Seckel 1968, 114), which is often separate from their content, can perform efficacious work without extra ritual activities such as recitation. If scriptures are accepted as iconic sacred beings, then their potency lies in their very presence. As such, it can be said that the efficacy of scriptures is based on and originates from the iconic dimension. Most lay Buddhists neither understand the content of scriptures nor do they perform rituals related to the content of what is written. Instead, they make the most of the iconic dimension of scriptures by utilizing their physical forms (see Watts 2006 [2008], 142).

By investigating the example of miniature sutras in Korea we will demonstrate that a scripture can perform work for adherents without explicit ritual performance, as long as the scripture has iconicity. For this purpose, we will first outline the historical background to the custom of storing sutras in the belly of Buddha statues, which will help understand how scriptures could be equated with dharma or the Buddha himself. Then we will focus on how miniature sutras work efficaciously within the belly of Buddha statues and in the hands or pockets of Buddhists.

Sutras changing statues into the living Buddha

From the early stages of Indian Buddhism, Buddhist scriptures have enjoyed sacred status that is equivalent to the Buddha himself. Scriptures have been equated with dharma, the basic doctrine and teachings of the Buddha. Dharma has simultaneously occupied a very peculiar and prominent place in Buddhism. Gautama Siddhartha became the Buddha after he discovered the dharma. According to the *Nirvana Sutra*, one of the early sutras, the Buddha advised his disciples to take the dharma as their guide after his death. In addition, dharma is the second of the "three jewels"

Powerful Tiny Scriptures

or refuges of Buddhists along with Buddha and sangha. Since cherishing and taking refuge in the three jewels is a primary criterion for being regarded as a Buddhist, it is clear that these three are important elements of Buddhism. The word dharma often designates sutras, the scriptural texts of the Buddha's teachings, and sometimes extends to mantras or *dharanis*, short spell-like texts thought to encapsulate various aspects of the Buddha's teachings. Furthermore, dharma is regarded as the essence of the Buddha himself. It is one of the two "bodies" that Mahayana Buddhism has distinguished in order to explain Buddha's embodiment in the scriptural traditions that recorded his teachings and in the physical form. According to Charles Willemen, "[t]he two bodies are the law-body (*dharmakaya*), which is the dharma, the essence of Buddha, and the material body (*rupakaya*), the physical aspect" (Willemen 2004, 219). The Buddha is the teacher of dharma and, at the same time, a personification of dharma.

We would like to emphasize again that sutras easily acquire iconic status independent of their semantic content because they are identified with dharma and therefore the Buddha. José Ignacio Cabezón correctly points out that "[Buddhist] scriptures cannot be reduced to their content or meaning, since they are put to many uses that have nothing to do with their meaning" and that "they serve as an object of worship and devotion" (Cabezón 2004, 757). The iconicity of Buddhist scriptures is founded on the religious notion that they are embodiments of dharma and the Buddha.

In the Buddhist traditions, scriptures came to be equated with relics of the Buddha and stored in stupas. In India, stupas were objects of worship because they contained relics called *sariras*, mainly ash, of a saintly person (Dallapiccola 2004, 803). With the spread of Buddhism, relics of the Buddha were laid in stupas in other countries that adopted the religion. Though it was a matter of course that the Buddha relics were limited, this practice could be widely followed because "the term 'relic' was interpreted very freely indeed, and was extended to include sacred texts (sutras) and spells (*dharanis*) as the word-body of the Buddha" (Seckel 1968, 114). Texts, which took various forms and were made of many different materials according to places and periods, such as birch bark, palm leaf, bamboo stalk, or paper, replaced the bodily remnants of the Buddha in stupas, effectively becoming relics themselves and making the stupas objects of worship. This practice illustrates how the iconicity of scriptures was separate from their content.

In Korea, scriptures were from the early eighth century stored in pagodas, which function as stupas in East Asia, in place of Buddha relics or symbolic substitutes such as beads and jewels. Though various sutras and *dharanis*, including the *Diamond Sutra, Flower Ornament Sutra, Pratityasamutpadagatha,* and *Cundi Mantra*, were placed in pagodas, *Great Dharani Sutra of Immaculate and Pure Light* was the most common text put in pagoda reliquaries (Ju 2016, 270). Early examples of miniature sutras are found in the pagodas built from approximately the eighth century to the twelfth century. Pagodas frequently contained within them miniature pagodas of 5 to 10 centimeters in height, which were made of wood, metals, stone, or clay (The National Museum of Korea 1991, 112-127).[1] Some of these miniature pagodas placed in the large pagodas were furnished with a hole in which a small *dharani* paper roll was inserted (Ju 2004, 171).

Buddha relics—understood, in a broad sense, to include sutras, *dharanis*, beads, or jewels—had been originally stored in stupas or pagodas. Gradually they came to be placed in the empty space of Buddha statues. Korean Buddhists have believed for centuries that statues become the real Buddha and come to have sacred power if relics are stored in them. This is called the belief in *saengsin* ("the living body") (Mun 1991). As there is a high possibility that Buddha relics were installed in the *ushnisha*, the topknot appearing on top of the head of the Buddha statues, in second- and third-century Gandhara (Rhi 2004, 134-146),[2] it would seem that the relics were installed within the Buddha statues in India from quite an early period. Relics were also stored in statues in China but none dating from before the tenth century. Some scholars argue that relics including scriptures began to be stored in statues in Korea from the late eighth century; the ground of a Vairocana Buddha statue made in 776 CE bears a trace of what might have been a reliquary ("Bokjang" 2010). Around ten statues with relics, belonging to the late Goryeo dynasty period (thirteenth to fourteenth centuries), have been discovered and there are hundreds of such relic-statues belonging to the Joseon dynasty (fifteenth to nineteenth centuries) (Jeontongbulbokjang 2014, 126). Besides scriptures and relics, ceremonial items, such as the five types of incense, medicine, and grain, the five colors of thread and cloth, as well as beads and other jewels, were also stored in the statues (Jeontongbulbokjang 2014, 134-137).[3]

---

1. Sometimes small pagoda images were engraved on metal plates or on the surface of the gilt bronze reliquaries (The National Museum of Korea 1991, 24, 113).
2. Buddha relics in China and Korea seem to have been sometimes stored in the heads of statues, rather than in the belly (Mun 1991). Recently, a copy of the *Mahaprajnaparamita Sutra* was found in the head of a Buddha statue in Silsangsa Temple (Namweon, South Korea). The statue is estimated to be from the late fourteenth century (Park 2017).
3. Korean Buddhism appears to have developed its own way of storing relics distinct from that of China. Relic containers in the shape of bottles and cylinders are not seen in Chinese Buddha statues, but were commonly used in Korea. In addition,

While the specific content varied, scriptures were the most important item, and were never excluded. It is clear that it was necessary to keep sutras – commonly *Lotus Sutra*, *Surangama Sutra*, *Diamond Sutra*, *Golden Light Sutra*, *Flower Ornament Sutra*, *Ksitigarbha Sutra*, and various kinds of *dharani*s written on paper—stored in the Buddha statues (Jeontongbulbokjang 2014, 118–125). The scriptures transformed the statues into "the living body" of the Buddha with their presence.

Miniature sutras working in Buddha's belly

The practice of storing scriptures in statues was primarily found in temples and collective places for worship. Today, however, many lay Buddhists in contemporary Korea have Buddha statues in their own homes. Though there are relatively large statues for domestic use whose height is about 60 centimeters, most are statues to be placed on desks or display cabinets and are about 20 centimeters in height. Like the small *dharani* scrolls inserted into miniature pagodas, these Buddha statues require miniature sutras in order to become "the living body" of the Buddha. The letters printed on the pages of these miniature books are too small to read. In addition, they are often printed in classical Chinese without Korean phonetic script or translation. It is clear that miniature sutras are specially made to transform the essence of the Buddha statues, and are not intended for study or recitation. They are accepted as representations of the dharma, regarded as having equivalent status to the Buddha, and make the statues become the real Buddha with power to bless and protect the possessors.

We are not arguing that Korean Buddhists do not care about the semantic dimension of scriptures. Some devout Korean lay Buddhists certainly put stress on the content of sutras and try to read and study them, which is proved clearly by the use of readable "mini-sutras" among Korean Buddhists. Korean Buddhist shops, both online and offline, sell mini-sutras, the purpose and usage of which can be divided into two types by size.[4]

Korean Buddhists did not install items such as cloth and thread arranged in the shape of internal organs, which was a common practice in China (Jeontongbulbokjang 2014, 101–108; Yi 2016, 94).

4. The authors visited two Buddhist shops and interviewed the owners on July 22, 2017. The two shops are "Bulsimweon" and "Taeseongbulgyosa," both of which are located in Jongro-gu, Seoul, near the Jogyesa Temple, the headquarters of the Jogye Order of Korean Buddhism. The authors also consulted the catalogs of ten online Buddhist shops for this research: Buddhazone (2008), available at: http://www.buddhazone.co.kr/shop/main/index.php. Accessed July 24, 2017; Bulgyomart (2012), available at: http://www.bulkyomart.com/. Accessed July 24, 2017; Bulgyosesang (2012), available at: http://www.bulkyosesang.co.kr/. Accessed July 24, 2017; Jongrobulgyosa (2012), available at: http://www.jongrobulkyosa.co.kr/index/index.php. Accessed July 24, 2017; Mahamall (1998), available at: http://www.mahamall.

The size of the first type is 6 to 8.5 centimeters wide and 11 to 13 centimeters long containing 150 to 200 pages. These scriptures are small pocket-sized books too large to be regarded as "miniature," are easy to carry, and are made to be read. These portable sutras clearly involve the semantic dimension of the scriptures as well as their iconic and performative dimensions. Most books in this category consist of two parts: The first part contains sutras written in classical Chinese characters with Korean endings and phonetic pronunciation in Korean script. This part is intended to provide the iconic and performative dimensions of scriptures. When lay Buddhists who do not know the meaning of the Chinese scripture recite what is written by reading Korean phonetic values, they expect to have the sacred power of the sutra. Furthermore, they intend to enjoy the protection and blessing of the Buddha by simply carrying these small books. The second part is a Korean interpretation of the classical Chinese text. Buddhists read this part to understand the teachings of the Buddha. The use of this part thus involves the semantic dimension. Many scriptures that have been popular in Korea for a long time, including the *Dhammapada, Lotus Sutra, Diamond Sutra, Flower Ornament Sutra, Heart Sutra, Thousand Hands Sutra, Avalokitesvara Sutra, The Sutra of the Medicine Buddha's Vows* and others, are published as pocketbooks for the laity who wants to carry and read the word-body of the Buddha at the same time.

On the other hand, this kind of mini-sutra takes another form that contains only the classical Chinese characters and their Korean transliteration, without the Korean translation. These pocketbooks are approximately of the same size, but have fewer pages in comparison to the mini-sutras that include translations. When using these mini-sutras, the semantic dimension is not present but the iconic and performative dimensions are indisputable. Lay Buddhists can easily carry and recite the part printed in Korean without understanding the meaning. In carrying these small scriptures and reciting them phonetically, Buddhists expect the scriptures to bless and protect them.

The mini-sutras of the second type are obvious miniatures that can involve both iconic and performative dimensions when they are used. It is almost impossible to read the smallest miniature sutras, which cover between 50 and 80 pages and measure just 2.3 centimeters in width and

---

co.kr/. Accessed July 24, 2017; Moranbulgyoyongpum (2006), available at: http://moranbulkyo.co.kr/index.html. Accessed July 24, 2017; Sabanuri (2010), available at: http://sabanuri.com/. Accessed July 24, 2017; Sachalmall (2005), available at: http://www.sachal.kr/. Accessed July 24, 2017; Sejonmall (2003), available at: http://www.sejonmall.com/FrontStore/iStartPage.phtml. Accessed July 24, 2017; Seonjaemall (2008), available at: http://www.seonjaemall.co.kr/. Accessed July 24, 2017.

Powerful Tiny Scriptures

Figure 6.1.Miniature sutras (left) and readable mini-sutras (right). Photo: author.

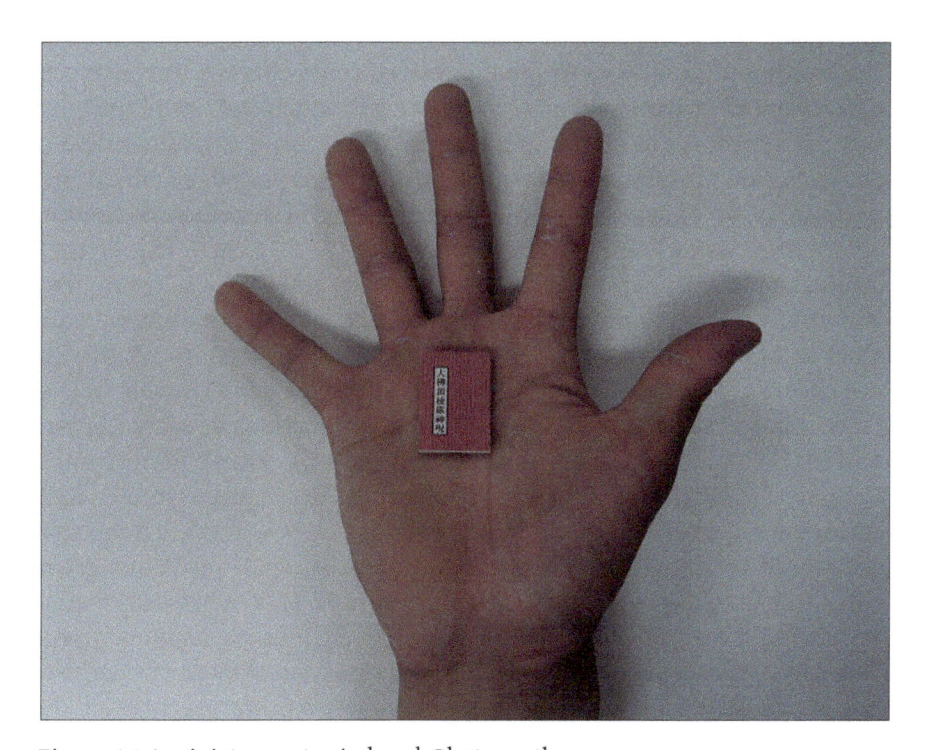

Figure 6.2.A miniature sutra in hand. Photo: author.

3.3 centimeters in length. It is also very difficult to read the slightly larger books, which tend to be 3.8 centimeters wide and 5.5 centimeters long. In addition, they usually do not have Korean transliteration or translation. It is clear that they are produced neither for study nor for recitation. These two sizes of miniature sutras are either stored in the small Buddha statues that are kept in the home or carried by Buddhists in their pockets or bags. Inside the Buddha statues, the miniatures are believed to put life into the statues and transform them into embodiments of the real Buddha, who blesses and helps the statues' owners in everyday life.

Lay Buddhists use these miniature sutras in ways that differ from those of monks or nuns in two respects: First, lay Buddhists do not consider the content of the sutras that they place in the statue at home. Rather, the iconic status of miniature sutras is independent of their semantic meaning. People usually purchase miniature sutras that they can easily obtain, most of which are concise and therefore easily made into miniatures, such as the *Heart Sutra, Diamond Sutra, Surangama Mantras*, the chapter of "Avalokitesvara's Universal Gate" of the *Lotus Sutra*, the *Thousand Hands Sutra*, the chapter of "Samantabhadra's Conduct and Vows" of the *Flower Ornament Sutra*, and the *Avalokitesvara Sutra*. However, the sacred status and power of a scripture that enabled it to replace the Buddha relics and the Buddha himself were originally related to its content. For instance, *Great Dharani Sutra of Immaculate and Pure Light*, which was one of the most popular scriptures to be put in the reliquaries of pagodas, as mentioned above, became favored by the royal family and was placed in many stupas because the text itself states that Heavenly Devas will protect the country where pagodas containing this sutra are built (Ju 2016, 267). This demonstrates that the iconic status and performative power of a scripture may be initially related to the semantic content and later become autonomous from it. Many Korean lay Buddhists also sometimes choose sutras that are known for their talismanic power, as will be explained further below.

Second, scriptures can perform distinctive functions as sacred beings within the Buddha statues without any specific ritual performance. Complicated rituals for installing Buddha relics or scriptures into Buddha statues were developed for Buddhist temples. As shown above, items that are stored in statues with scriptures such as incense, medicine, grain, thread, and beads, are related to temple ceremonies. Even nowadays, some people put a very small amount of grain, thread, incense, and tiny plastic beads in statues along with miniature scriptures, but they do not perform any particular rituals when installing these items in statues. Instead, the items are purchased in small pre-packed boxed sets at Buddhist shops

Powerful Tiny Scriptures

Figure 6.3. Items including miniature sutras that are stored in domestic small Buddha statues. Photo: author.

Figure 6.4. Inserting the box that includes miniature sutras into a small Buddha statue. Photo: author. Sutras Working in Buddhists' Pockets.

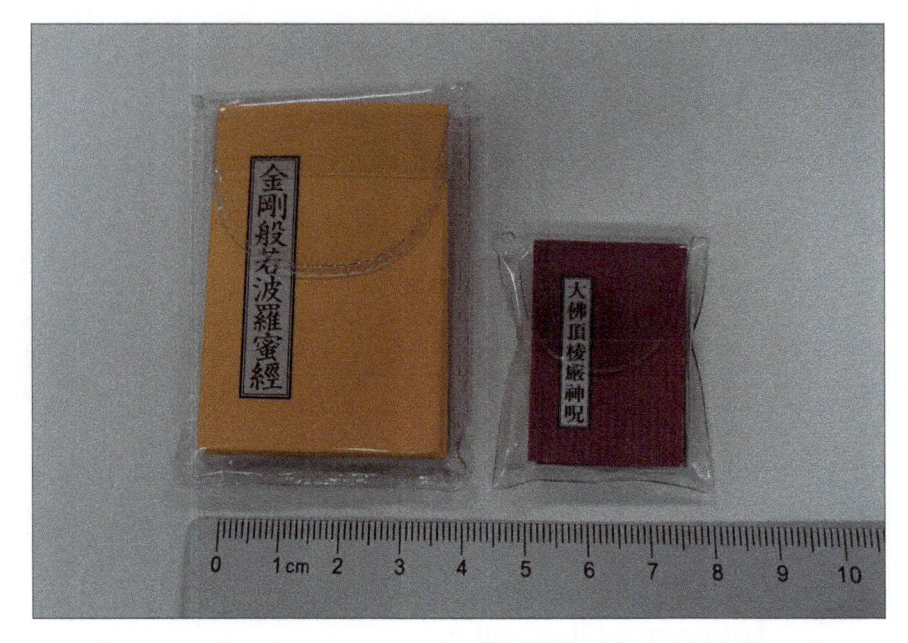

Figure 6.5. *Hosinyong* miniature sutras carried in purses or bags. Photo: author.

and placed all at once into the hole at the bottom of a Buddha statue. Sometimes a small *dharani* or *mandala* scroll that is included for free when purchasing a statue is attached with glue at the bottom to seal the hole after the items are inserted. Though this process may be regarded as a ritual in a broad sense, there is no conscious ritual performance carried out at home. For further convenience, statues for purchase also have the scriptures or the small box pre-installed. The procedure in which scriptures and other items are stored does not appear to be important to lay Buddhists who possess the statue. Rather, the scriptures are believed to have iconicity that can activate the statues and turn them into the Buddha himself not by specific ritual performances but simply by the presence of small scriptures.

The power of sutras has been recognized and appropriated in the whole Buddhist cultural landscape. Because the dharma is considered "the protector" of people (Willemen 2004, 219), sutras are believed to protect their readers, listeners, and possessors. Shorter mantras and *dharanis* are more easily recited and can be efficiently used for helping Buddhists in various contexts. When these short texts are chanted, they are believed to help lay Buddhists "achieve the material blessings and protections needed for a good worldly life" (Esposito, Fasching, and Lewis 2015, 428). The sacred status and power of sutras as dharma and the Buddha are recognized and

Powerful Tiny Scriptures

appropriated not only by the laity, to most of whom the semantic dimension of the scriptures is unavailable, but also by monks and nuns who learn to read the sutras and understand their content. In all countries where Buddhism is prevalent, monks and nuns generally engage in practices and rites based on the iconic and performative dimensions of scriptures.

Though scholars of religious texts have mostly limited their research to the semantic dimension of scriptures, academics have also highlighted the performative functions of scriptures when reading, reciting, or otherwise repeating them (Graham 1987; Levering 1989). For instance, Miriam Levering explored the functions of sutras in a Buddhist convent in contemporary Taiwan (Levering 1989, 72–90). The Taiwanese nuns of this convent believed that the sacred words of the scriptures recited in rituals protected people and brought benefits to them. In addition, according to Levering, the nuns recited and copied sutras because they believed that by doing so they could eliminate the past accumulation of negative karma (Levering 1989, 73). Other scholars have shown how certain Buddhist rituals materialize the power gained by reading or reciting sutras. A popular world religions textbook introduces the Buddhist ritual of making water imbued with powers of chanted sutras:

> In the simplest (and still most popular) universal Buddhist ritual, monks pour water into a vessel as they chant words revealed by the Buddha. Now imbued with healing powers, the liquid can be drunk or sprinkled over the bodies of those needing assistance. (Esposito, Fasching, and Lewis 2015, 446)

But it should be remembered that ritual reciting or chanting does not explain the whole non-semantic dimension of scriptures. Ritual performances are not necessarily required in order to activate the sacred power of scriptures. Scriptures can have a beneficial effect just by being held in the hands or kept in purses. In this sense, José Ignacio Cabezón likens scriptures to amulets and talismans, which are kept or worn "as a way of protecting the bearers or consumers of the text from evil or harm" (Cabezón 2004, 757). In Korea, many kinds of sutras, both those in book form and those with the text printed on other types of material items, are manufactured and displayed at home (see Chapter 2). But miniature sutras are the easiest to wear or carry and consequently considered to be the most effective means to protect the wearers or bearers without requiring any specific ritual performance.

In online Buddhist shops, the miniature sutras that measure 2.3 by 3.3 centimeters or 3.8 by 5.5 centimeters are dubbed *bokjangyong,* which means "for storing in the Buddha statues," and *hosinyong,* meaning "for self-protection." The same tiny books that transform statues into the liv-

Figure 6.6. Miniature sutras for key chains or cellphones. Photo: author.

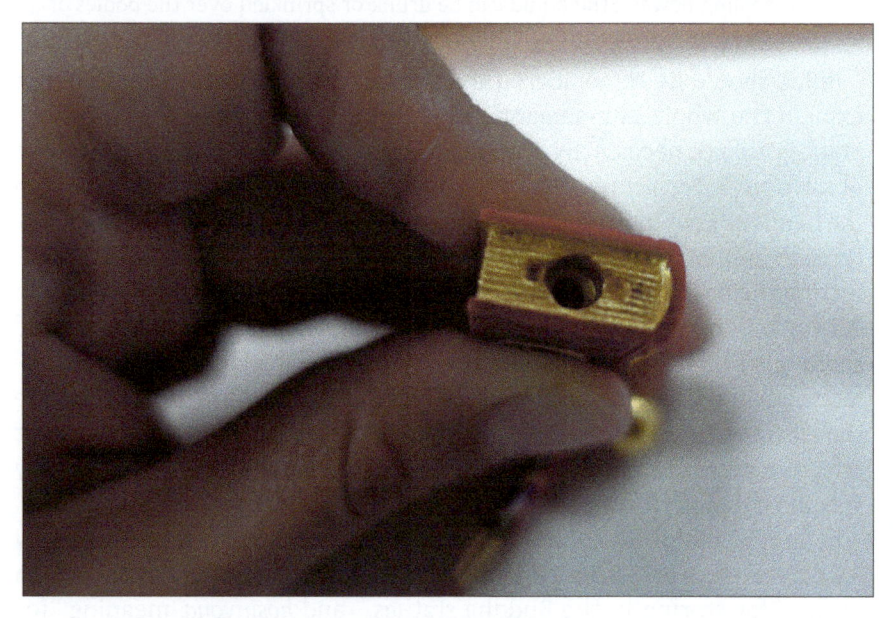

Figure 6.7. A plastic box miniature sutra with a hole into which a paper scroll sutra is inserted. Photo: author.

ing Buddha are thus also believed to protect people who carry them from the evil in the world. They are usually placed in protective plastic covers and carried in purses or bags. In addition, *hosinyong* miniature sutras are often made into accessories to be attached to a key chain, cellphone, or the rearview mirror of a car. Wherever the bearers may go, they can be protected by the miniature sutra, or the word-body of the Buddha. A type of miniature sutra in a contemporary printed codex that can be used for this purpose is available in Buddhist shops. It is a very small book, measuring 3.5 centimeters in width and 5 centimeters in length, and has a plastic cover that looks like leather, with the pages embossed in gold. It is a real book although the letters in it are too small to read. The manufacturer of this accessory miniature book is ambitious, cramming the *Thousand Hands Sutra*, the *Heart Sutra*, the *Diamond Sutra*, "Samantabhadra's Conduct and Vows" of the *Flower Ornament Sutra*, the *Avalokitesvara Sutra*, and several prayers into the tiny tome. But as this book is fragile, more people prefer to carry a plastic replica of scriptures that measures 1.7 centimeters wide, 2.8 centimeters long, and 0.5 centimeters deep. The replica is a small box that looks like a book on which the title of a sutra is engraved. At the bottom of this book-shaped box there is a tiny hole in which a real text written on a small paper scroll is inserted. Concise sutras, like the *Diamond Sutra* or the chapter "Avalokitesvara's Universal Gate" of the *Lotus Sutra*, are used for this miniature text inside a miniature replica sutra. This light and strong plastic miniature is very suitable for key chains or cellphone cases.

Buddhists have thus believed that sutras can protect and bless their possessors and bearers. Miniature sutras are made to fulfill this function most effectively because they can be worn or carried very easily. The uses of these small sutras involve only their iconic dimension since the books are too small to read and they are believed to possess powers independent of their semantic content and any recitation or repetition of what is written in them. Even if the users do not understand their meaning and do not perform any specific rituals, the miniature sutras are believed to exert sacred power by being present as sacred beings.

Conclusion

From the beginning of Buddhist history, scriptures have been identified with dharma, one of the three refuges of Buddhists, and they have enjoyed sacred status as an embodiment of the Buddha himself. This status of scriptures as sacred beings involves their iconic dimension since the scriptures are recontextualized in various situations of everyday life and rituals in which understanding their semantic content is not given preference.

Lay Buddhists especially believe the use of scriptures can be efficacious irrespective of their content and without any specific ritual performance. When a scripture, which is an expression of dharma and therefore the Buddha himself, is stored in a Buddha statue, the statue is believed to become the living body of the Buddha. In the hands or purses of Buddhists, it is handled more like an amulet or talisman that is believed to bless them and protect them from the evil.

Though Buddhists have thought of and treated their religious scriptures as sacred beings for a long time, they have also developed various new ways of appropriating the power of scriptures more efficiently. The use of miniature sutras in contemporary Korea is a new means of mobilizing the power of scriptures. Because they are easy to obtain and carry, they can work within small Buddha statues on a desk at home, or can accompany users everywhere while attached to a rearview mirror, cellphone, or key chain. Though it is very difficult and sometimes impossible to read these small miniature sutras, for most of their users it does not matter. As long as the iconicity of a miniature sutra is recognized, it can work as a sacred being even if the possessors do not read or understand its content.

7

SCRIPTURES FOR RECITATION IN DONGHAK (EASTERN LEARNING)

The "Theo-praxy" of Donghak as manifested in reciting scriptures

In this chapter, I will show how the semantic and the performative dimensions of scriptures are ritualized together in the recitation of the two scriptures of Donghak, the *Donggyeongdaejeon* and the *Yongdamyusa*. All Donghak members were required to memorize and recite only a brief incantation taken from *Donggyeongdaejeon*. While the incantation, which is composed of twenty-one Chinese characters, had to be repeated continuously, it was also necessary for members to understand what it meant. Scholars of Donghak have stressed the importance of the incantation. For instance, it has been described as "what implicatively contains the teaching of the founder, namely, all the doctrines" of Donghak (Yun and Hong 2016, 50) or as "what summarizes essential values and contents in the form of language" (Choi 2009b, 153). Considering that the second leader of Donghak called the incantation "the text of heaven"[天書] (see further below), it can be understood as a compressed version of all of the Donghak scriptures (Yun and Hong 2016, 167).

Though Donghak members were not asked to memorize and recite the second book, the *Yongdamyusa* which was composed in Korean verse, many members did so because its genre, *gasa*, was made to be metrically recited. *Gasa* works included in the *Yongdamyusa* as chapters were enjoyed through recitation. Members could understand the contents of the *Yongdamyusa* easily because this scripture was composed in the colloquial language of the public. In this last chapter, therefore, we see an example of the performance of reciting the incantation intermingling with the semantic dimension of the text, both intentionally and unintentionally.

The Korean new religion, Donghak (Eastern Learning)

Since most English-speaking readers will never have heard of Donghak, I will provide a general introduction to this religion before I articulate characteristics of reciting Donghak scriptures. Donghak is a new Korean religion founded by Jeu Choe (1824-1864), whose *nom de plume* is Suun, in 1860.[1] The religion's name can be literally translated as "Eastern (*dong*) Learning (*hak*)." The second part of the term, "hak," is directly translated into English as learning or studies but can also mean a religious tradition that has its own doctrines and practices (Yun and Hong 2016, 29).[2] By establishing this new Korean religion, Suun intended to oppose "*Seohak*," which can be translated as "Western Learning" and referred at that time to Roman Catholicism in Korea. His new religion is reported to be based on his own intense religious experience of meeting *hanalnim*, a Korean word that can be translated into English as the Heavenly Lord and which designated the highest god of the universe. He also tried to accept and appropriate the traditional religious ideas of East Asia, namely, Confucianism, Buddhism, and Daoism, in his new religious movement.

In 1905, Byeonghui Son, the third leader of the community, changed the name Donghak to its current name, Cheondogyo, literally meaning "Religion of the Heavenly Way." The name Donghak is currently not used to indicate active religious denominations that originated from the religion Suun founded. Cheondogyo has maintained its status as the mainstream sect derived from Donghak, while a few minor sects whose members consider themselves as heirs of Donghak also remain. One small sect cherishes the title Donghak in its own name of "Donghakgyo," which means "the religion of Donghak" (Choi 2009b, 221-227). Though the influence of Cheondogyo is not as significant nowadays as before, the religion was recognized as one of the representative national religions during the Japanese colonial period (1910-1945) and made its mark in Korean history by actively participating in the Korean independence movement from Japan.

Studies on Donghak have been focused on its doctrines and ideas while its practices have been relatively overlooked. To overcome this tendency,

---

1. The name of the second leader of Donghank, the successor of Jeu Choe, is Sihyeong Choe. Though they had the same last name and were known to be distant relatives, they were not from the same family. To avoid confusion between them, I will use the *nom de plume* Suun to indicate the founder Jeu Choe and use the *nom de plume* Haewol for his successor Sihyeong Choe.

2. Before the term *jong-gyo* [宗敎], the translated word for religion in Chinese characters, began to be circulated in East Asia from the late nineteenth century, *hak* [學], along with *gyo* [敎], *do* [道], *jong* [宗], was used for indicating religious teachings and practices. See Cho 2018, 142.

Scriptures for Recitation in Donghak

Jongseong Choi adeptly suggests that the term "theo-praxy" should be used to describe the characteristics of Donghak, to help understand that this tradition's theology and practices are inseparably united (Choi 2009b, 61–62). Accepting the term suggested by Choi, I argue that the theo-praxy of Donghak is revealed most clearly in the recitation of the two scriptures, the *Donggyeongdaejeon* and the *Yongdamyusa*. Cheondogyo and other sects derived from the early Donghak movement acknowledge as canonical scriptures only these two books written by the founder Suun, whom they recognize as the Great Sacred Teacher, while texts authored by the second or the third leaders are regarded as "authoritative teachings."

Suun and the two scriptures

The name *Donggyeongdaejeon* means "the complete collection of Donghak scripture" and *Yongdamyusa* can be translated as "songs (or poems) left by Suun." Yongdam, the first half of the book title, is the name of the place where Suun is believed to have met God and so where Donghak first began. It also designates Suun himself as a metonymy (Donghakhakhoe

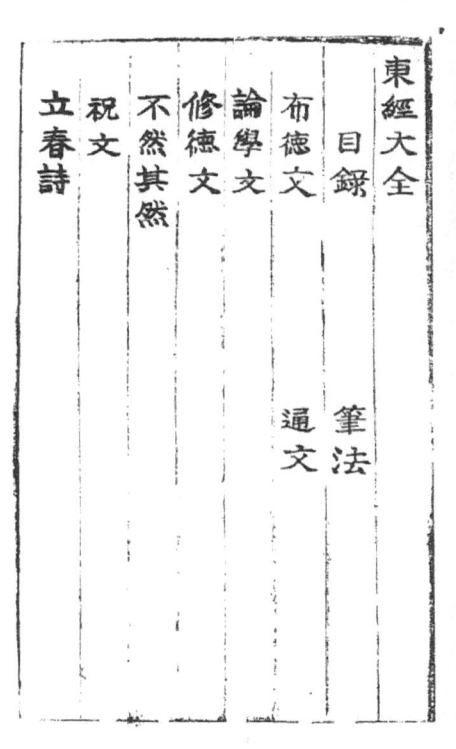

東經大全　布德目錄　論學文　修德文　不然其然　祝文　立春詩　　筆法　遍文

Figure 7.1. The contents page of the 1883 edition of *Donggyeongdaejeon*. Photo: author.

2009, 50). The two scriptures were published more than fifteen years after Suun's execution in 1864. The *Donggyeongdaejeon* was first published in book form in 1880 and the *Yongdamyusa* in 1881 by the second leader of Donghak, though the earliest surviving versions were published in 1883 (Yun 2009, 13). The second leader Sihyeong Choe (1827-1898), whose *nom de plume* is Haewol, gathered the writings of his teacher Suun, which had been handed down separately since Suun's death. Haewol collected and published Suun's writings in classical Chinese as the *Donggyeongdaejeon* and his writings in Korean as the *Yongdamyusa* (Yun and Hong 2016, 53-54; Donghakhakhoe 2001, 34-35, 82).

While Korean was the spoken language in the Joseon dynasty (1392-1910), written languages were more complicated. From a young age, men of the noble class were expected to learn classical Chinese to read Confucian texts, unless their family was too poor to educate them. They monopolized writing and reading in classical Chinese and were also able to read and write in the Korean alphabet, *Hangeul*, which was much easier to learn and use than the thousands of ideographic Chinese characters. Most men from the commoner class and many aristocratic women are thought not to have been able to read and write in classical Chinese. There were many more people who could not read and write even in Korean than those who could. According to the first census investigating literacy rates, which was taken by the Japanese colonial government in 1930, 69.9 percent of Koreans above the age of fifteen were not able to read or write in Korean or Japanese. We can guess that the illiteracy rate was higher when Suun wrote the Donghak scriptures around 1860, because 79 percent of Koreans who were above sixty years old in 1930 could not read or write Korean (KOSIS 2007). In Donghak's early years, for most members of the general public, scriptures were not for reading or writing. Early members were expected to recite only the brief incantation included in the *Donggyeongdaejeon* using Korean phonetic values. The *Yongdamyusa* that was composed in Korean was originally created not to be read, but to be orally learned and recited.

Suun wrote in the *Donggyeongdaejeon* that he first heard the voice of the god of heaven ordering him to spread his will in April 1860 of the lunar calendar. This mysterious experience is extremely important in Donghak as it marks the beginning of the new religion. According to the early history of Donghak compiled under the leadership of Haewol, even before this mysterious experience there were auspicious signs indicating that Suun would become the Great Sacred Teacher and spread God's will in this world (Choe 2000, 19-25). For instance, in 1855, an old Buddhist monk whom Suun later recognized as a divine person, gave him a book of heaven that taught Suun

Figure 7.2. Yongdam pavilion rebuilt in 1975 by Cheondogyo. The area surrounding this building is a holy site for Cheondogyo. Photo: Jongseong Choi.

how to pray and make contact with God. After devoting himself to praying at Cheonseong mountain in the Yangsan area of the Gyeongsang province in 1856 and 1857, he came back to his hometown of Gyeongju in October 1859. He confined himself in a small building called Yongdam, which his deceased father used as a study and where he met God the following year (Choi and Park 2020, 53–54). He began to write pieces of verse in Korean from the second half of 1860. The last work included in the *Yongdamyusa* is thought to have been written in August 1863. Chinese writings included in the *Donggyeongdaejeon* were composed between spring 1861, the year he began mission work, and November 1863, one month before his arrest by the Joseon government.

The *Donggyeongdaejeon*, which was written in classical Chinese, contains four chapters in prose, twenty-four brief poems and aphorisms, and the incantation (*jumun*), which can also be translated as "prayer." This scripture is composed of about 6,500 Chinese characters. Suun wrote about his mysterious experience and religious thoughts in the four prose pieces, three of which deal with the incantation in detail. Among the three pieces, "Podeokmun" (525 characters), "Nonhakmun" (1,338 characters), and "Sudeokmun" (1,060 characters), the meaning and significance of the incantation is most elaborately expounded in "Nonhakmun." Suun not only describes receiving the incantation from the god, *Hanalnim*, who can be translated as the Heavenly Lord and designates the highest god, but also suggests a quite detailed exposition of its meaning.

The *Yongdamyusa* contains eight quite long pieces composed in verse, written in the colloquial Korean of the time so that the common people could understand and recite it without difficulty. Suun vividly expressed his own deep emotions, both agonies and joys, in those pieces in Korean, his own mother language. He created one more piece in verse, whose original Korean version has not been passed down but whose Chinese version, which was translated by a government official when Suun was interrogated, has remained. In light of the fact that the pieces in Korean verse in the *Yongdamyusa* began to be written before the Chinese works in the *Donggyeongdaejeon*, the elaborate theological and cosmological ideas contained in the *Donggyeongdaejeon* in Chinese seem to have been developed from the Korean pieces in the *Yongdamyusa*. Though the first printed edition of the *Yongdamyusa* was published only in 1881, Donghak members had memorized and recited those pieces from the time Suun was active before his execution. Parts of the *Yongdamyusa* were made for and circulated by recitation, which I will explain further in the latter part of this chapter.

If one compares the length of the two scriptures, the *Yongdamyusa* containing 14,000 Korean characters seems to be approximately twice as long as the *Donggyeongdaejeon* that has 6,500 Chinese characters. However, a simple comparison of their length is deceptive, mainly due to the ideographic nature of Chinese writing, while alphabetic writing must use multiple signs for the more polysyllabic Korean words. Nevertheless, it still shows that Suun seemed to develop his ideas unconstrainedly in his own language while he tried to make his points more clearly and briefly in Chinese.

While these two books reveal the doctrines and thoughts of the founder that were inherited by his successors, they were made for the purpose of self-cultivation and were seen as the most important means of self-cultivation. Self-cultivation is one of the two main categories of Donghak practices, as is seen in Choi's classification of Donghak practices into ritual offerings and self-cultivation (Choi 2009, 113). While the founder tried to commune with God through ritual offerings, he also strongly emphasized self-cultivation for followers which he asserted can be practiced especially by reciting the incantation or prayer included in the *Donggyeongdaejeon*. From the beginning, the recitation of the incantation, which is believed to summarize the whole scripture, was the most important practice of the followers. The book of *Yongdamyusa* itself cannot be separated from the activity of recitation. It is comprised of nine pieces called *gasa*, a traditional Korean poetic genre meant to be recited aloud.

Scriptures for Recitation in Donghak

Reciting the scriptures was critical for the development of early Donghak and constituted the identity of its early participants. The recitation was the most emphasized ritual way for serving God, and played an important role in teaching and publicizing the core myths and doctrines of the movement. The recitation of the incantation included in the *Donggyeongdaejeon*, which is believed to be the core and summary of not only the book but of Donghak itself, was the most important means to practice self-cultivation. Only those who recited the incantation were entitled to be members of Donghak, just as Muslims should recite the *Shahada* (confession of faith). Many of the first devotees took so much pleasure in reciting the *Yongdamyusa* that they came to memorize the whole book.

Researchers on Donghak scriptures have mainly focused on interpreting and explaining their contents. Though it has been recognized that the recitation of the incantation is mandatory for being a member of Donghak and that *gasa*, the poetic genre of the *Yongdamyusa*, was made and circulated for recitation, the importance of the recitation of the scriptures in Donghak has not been sufficiently emphasized in academia. In this chapter, I will demonstrate the significance and function of reciting scriptures in Donghak by paying special attention to the interaction between the semantic dimension and the performative dimension of scripture, which is witnessed when the sacred texts of Donghak are recited. In the following sections, I will first examine the meaning of the incantation included in the *Donggyeongdaejeon*, articulating the importance of its recitation both for serving God and for self-cultivation. Then I will argue that the *Yongdamyusa* was made and used for indoctrinating early members by having them recite it. It will be shown that the sacred texts of Donghak became efficacious by being recited and that the contents and the performance of the scriptures are inseparably united in their recitation.

The incantation included and emphasized in Donghak scriptures

I would like to begin this section by emphasizing again that the incantation was at the center of Donghak members' lives and that it was regarded as the essence of the scriptures. Every member of Donghak was required to memorize and continuously recite it. The *Donggyengdaejeon* not only contains the incantation itself but also expounds upon it. Suun wrote that he received it from God, along with the sacred talisman that would be efficacious in healing followers from diseases. While the talisman has been practically unused since Suun's death[3] about four years after the first revelation, the incantation is still the core of faith and practice for

---

3. The talisman was rarely used after Suun's death in Donghak and Cheondogyo, though

the religious communities derived from Donghak. Suun must have put more stress on the incantation than the talisman, because many pages of the *Donggyeongdaejeon* are devoted to explaining the incantation whereas the talisman is very briefly treated. The scripture carries the incantation, interprets it, expounds it, and articulates its importance repeatedly. Most early members of Donghak who could not read or recite the scripture written in classical Chinese were supposed to recite the short incantation composed of twenty-one Chinese characters in Korean phonetic values.

It is not extraordinary that an incantation is the root and essence of a scripture, or even that the scripture is reckoned as the interpretation of the incantation. We can find similar examples in other religions. In the Indian tradition, a mantra is often looked upon as the essence and root of a holy text. According to C. Mackenzie Brown, some Purāṇic texts contain explicit self-interpretations that the root of the text is a mantra. The *Devī Bhāgavata Purāna* explains that "it originated in a half-verse mantra spoken by the Devī (Goddess) herself. The full text is simply an explanation of this root mantra" (Brown 1986, 75). A mantra is believed to be a living representative or the sound form of a deity. Therefore, a holy book that contains the mantra can make the deity visible and it can be said that the holy book is a visible manifestation of the deity (Watts and Yoo 2021, 3; Brown 1986, 81). This Indian view—that a holy text was originated in a mantra and that the text is an explanation of the mantra—demonstrates that a brief incantation can be identified with the essence and the root of the whole holy text. Likewise, the incantation is believed to be the essence of the *Donggyeongdaejeon*. Suun not only explains it word by word and suggests theological and philosophical interpretation of it, but also illustrates vividly how he received it from God and elaborated on it in language. In addition, taking the opportunity of comparing Indian texts with Donghak scriptures, I would like to mention that just as in Purāṇic texts, "there is evidence of an early complementary relationship between meaning and sound" (Brown 1986, 74). The meaning and the recitation of the Donghak incantation worked in complementary ways to ritualize the text. Though the incantation might seem to be recited by rote, its semantic dimension was also emphasized, first for elite members who knew classical Chinese and later for general members who were also supposed to study its meaning, which I will explain in greater detail later.

Here, I am focusing on the relationship between the scriptures and the incantation in Donghak. The *Donggyeongdaejeon* was designed to succinctly

---

some small sects that claimed to inherit Donghak, including Sangjegyo and Cheonjingyo, are reported to have used it.

convey the basic doctrines and thoughts of Donghak in classical Chinese, the language of the elite of the time. The incantation, which is included in the book, is a brief summary of the newly founded sect's core doctrines. It was recited during Donghak rituals and still is recited in Cheondogyo services, just as the Apostles' Creed and the Lord's Prayer are recited in Christian worship services. Reciting the incantation was a way of affirming Donghak members' identification with the sect, in a way that was typical of other new religious movements founded during the Joseon dynasty.

Members believed that reciting the incantation was a way of reifying the core doctrine of "sicheonju," which literally means "serving God." It is assumed that some early elite members recited not only the incantation but also the whole *Donggyeongdaejeon* for the purpose of studying the scripture. This was the case with Confucian students of the time, for whom recitation was the most common way of studying books. However, it was impossible for most members who could not read and write in Chinese to recite the whole scripture. All the members had to do was to recite the phonetic value of the incantation composed of twenty-one Chinese characters.

The composition of the early Donghak incantation was more complex than this single twenty-one letter incantation. The *Donggyeongdaejeon* includes two sets of incantations: Seonsaengjumun, which can be translated as the incantation of the teacher, and Jejajumun, which means the incantation of the disciples. Seonsaengjumun, composed of 19 Chinese characters, was to be recited only by Suun, the sacred teacher himself, and has not been used after Suun died. Jejajumun was a little longer because there were two steps in it. The first one was Chohakjumun, the incantation for the new members who were asked to recite it before and during their initiation rite. This part has not been used since the leadership of Haewol ended after his death (Jeong 2006, 222). The second part of Jejajumun is the incantation of twenty-one characters that are equated with the Donghak incantation itself. According to the early history book published by Haewol, "What Suun taught was only twenty-one characters" (Choe 2000 [1879], 45). Suun emphasized that all the contents of Donghak were contained in only the twenty-one characters. The only requirement to become a member was also to accept and recite the twenty-one-character incantation. This incantation also consists of two parts: eight characters of Gangryeongjumun, the incantation for receiving the spirit of the god, and thirteen characters of Bonjumnu, the main incantation. Gangryeongjumun can be translated as "May the utmost spirit of God come down to me." Bonjumun can be understood as "Serve God and you will be in harmony, do not forget God forever and you will be enlightened about everything" or "I would like to be in harmony by serving God and to be enlightened about everything by not forgetting God forever" (Choi 2009b, 153). As I wrote above, *jumun*, which is usually understood as incantation, can also be translated as prayer. Donghak members prayed that the spirit of God and their own be united by reciting Gangryeongjumun and that they serve and remember God always by reciting Bonjumun (Yun and Hong 2016, 50).

Suun himself often identified the second part of Jejajumun with the Donghak incantation itself, using the expression of "twenty-one-character incantation." In the *Donggyeongdaejeon*, the phrase "twenty-one characters" is repeated to designate this incantation. In "Dosusa" also included in the *Yongdamyusa*, the incantation is described in Korean as the twenty-one-character incantation (Choe 2009 [1881], 450). The early history book of Donghak records that the incantation was emphasized and performed from the beginning of Donghak (Choe 2000 [1879], 39). This is confirmed in the Annals of the Joseon Dynasty (*Joseonwangjosillok*). When Suun was arrested on the charge of deluding and deceiving the people, government officials estimated the sphere of Donghak influence by checking the area where the incantation was recited. When royal secretary Ungwi Jeong reported to King Gojong about the prevalence of Donghak, he mentioned the incantation.

> From Joryeong to Gyeongju [the area of the northern Gyeongsang province, where Suun began his mission work], I could hear about the story of Donghak almost every day. From women working at taverns to children in the remote countryside, so many people recite the incantation, saying 'wicheonju' [devoting to God, the first part of Chohakjumun] or 'sicheonju' [serving God, the first part of the twenty-one-character incantation]." (*Gojongsillok* book 1)

The incantation spread rapidly among the public when Donghak was propagated, as is seen by the fact that the government officials identified it as the conspicuous characteristic of Donghak.

Suun was not only the author and interpreter of the incantation, but also its first propagator. He repeatedly emphasizes its importance in the two scriptures. It was in "Podeokmun," the first chapter of the *Donggyeongdaejeon*, that he articulates the divine origin of the incantation. According to Suun, in the first meeting with God, God gave him the incantation and ordered him to teach it to people (Choe 2009 [1880], 35–36; Yun and Hong 2016, 275). God himself made it clear that people can serve and devote themselves to God through the incantation. Suun wrote that he received the incantation from God but also that he elaborately composed it. According to Suun, though it was God who inspired him and taught the truth contained in the incantation, it was his job to compose it in language.

In "Nonhakmun," the second chapter of the *Donggyeongdaejeon*, Suun wrote that it took one year for him to compose the incantation. He suggested in it the way for people to invite God and to remember God. He also asserted that the process of cultivating oneself is contained in the twenty-one characters (Choe 2009 [1880], 77-78). Among the eighteen paragraphs of "Nonhakmun," as separated by Seoksan Yun,[4] Suun devotes twelve paragraphs to explaining basic Donghak doctrines, including theology, cosmology, and anthropology, in the form of a conversation between himself and his disciples, whom he called "wise scholars." In three of the twelve paragraphs, he deals with the incantation, first articulating its significance and then expounding it word by word. According to "Sudeokmun," the third chapter of the *Donggyeongdaejeon*, Donghak members recited the twenty-one-character incantation from the beginning of Suun's mission work (Choe 2009 [1880], 149). In this chapter, Suun also emphasizes the importance of the incantation for members to cultivate themselves (153, 159).

The *Yongdamyusa*, written in Korean verse, does not contain the incantation written in Chinese, though Suun says that God ordered him to write a composition (Choe 2009 [1881], 330) which is often understood as the written works included in the two scriptures, but may also indicate the incantation. In this Korean scripture, Suun directly mentions the incantation only twice. First in "Gyohunga," which is estimated to be written in November or December in 1861, he asserts that if a person recites the incantation with his or her utmost sincerity, he or she will become wise and will not need all the books of the world (Choe 2009 [1881], 358). Here, Suun does not call the incantation twenty-one characters but rather thirteen characters, which corresponds to Bonjumnu, the second part of the twenty-one character incantation. Suun once more used "thirteen characters" to refer to the incantation itself in "Heungbiga," *Yongdamyusa* (Choe 2009 [1881], 504). I will explain further about this reduction of the number of characters later. Second, in "Dosusa," which is thought to be written in December 1861, Suun mentions the incantation when he summarizes his mission work as elaborating on the endless great way of Donghak [무극대도] and spreading the twenty-one characters to people of the world (Choe 2009 [1881], 450). This phrase implies that people can achieve the great way of Donghak by reciting the incantation, without having to make desperate efforts. The importance of the incantation is emphasized in the *Yongdamyusa*, if not as strongly as in the *Donggyeongdaejeon*.

---

4. Note that there are no separate paragraphs in Suun's original work. These paragraphs are separated by Seoksan Yun for the purpose of providing exegeses on "Nonhakmun." See Yun's annotation in Choe 2009 [1880], 59-126.

The incantation as the text of heaven

According to the *Donggyeongdaejeon*, God gave the incantation to Suun and designated it as the way people serve God. As I wrote above, it should be noted that *jumun* [주문], which corresponds to the English word incantation, can also be translated and understood as a prayer (Donghakhakhoe 2001, 40). Donghak members recited it for the purpose of serving the god and being united with God (Yun and Hong 2016, 206). Members were supposed to recite it devoutly, remembering always that God abides in them. They believed that they could develop a friendly relationship with God by reciting it (Jeong 2006, 222). Specifically, the incantation was regarded as words of God, words from God, words for God, and words through which people can approach God.

The power of the incantation is based on its divine origin, which is claimed in the two scriptures. And its authority cannot be imagined without its relation to the scriptures. The incantation is included, explained, interpreted, and repeatedly emphasized in both the *Donggyeongdaejeon* and the *Yongdamyusa*. Scriptures are "the most important symbol of power" (Wimbush 2012, 163), especially in religious communities that believe deities talk and act through scriptures. As I wrote in Chapter 5, scriptures are regarded as relevant, cryptic, and perfect when religious people believe scriptures come from God/gods. These scriptures often "convey mysterious power that has its origin in another realm—from God—and that can be employed to influence others" (Wimbush 2012, 177).

The whole Donghak scriptures were not believed to have come directly from God. Though Suun was accepted as the Great Sacred Teacher by members, it was also true that Suun expressed his own feelings, like joy and anguish, in the scriptures. But the scriptures attest that Suun received the incantation from God and included and emphasized this in them. Though the scriptures were written by the sacred teacher and so they are sacred books, the incantation was considered to be obviously from God and to yield special power "that has its origin in another realm," as Wimbush put it (2012, 177). The second leader, Haewol, further clarified that the incantation had come from God by defining the twenty-one characters as "the text of heaven" (Yun and Hong 2016, 167). While two scriptures are teachings and songs of the founder and the Great Sacred Teacher Suun, the incantation, a small part of the *Donggyeongdaejeon*, was believed to be the words of God and the text of heaven. In the next section, I will examine Suun's notion of the "god" who he believed gave him the incantation.

Reciting the Incantation for Serving God

From the beginning of this chapter, I have used the word "God" to indicate the being whom Suun believed he met and with whom Donghak members expected to unite. Here, the notion of God in Donghak should be explained briefly. In the *Donggyeongdaejeon*, Suun used words the *sangje* [上帝] or *cheonju* [天主] to refer to the being who gave him the incantation. The former is the name indicating in ancient China and Korea the heavenly supreme god who supervises all things in the universe. The latter is not only the name Chinese and Korean Catholics use for God but also the translation of the Korean word *hanalnim* into Chinese (Yun and Hong 2016, 78).[5] By using these Chinese words, Suun made it clear that the being who ordered him to do mission work was the one transcendental God (Donghakhakhoe 2001, 36-37). Though Suun used the word *sangje* several times in the *Yongdamyusa* in the Korean alphabet (Choe 2009 [1881], 366, 373, 486), he chose the Korean word *hanalnim* more often in the Korean scripture (Choe 2009 [1881], 324, 329, 337, 357, 371, 376, 381, 406, 494, 504, etc.). As I wrote above, *hanalnim* can be translated into English as the Heavenly Lord and be safely understood to designate the highest god of the universe.

It is said that Donghak began with Suun's religious experience of meeting God (Yun and Hong 2016, 35). This god is a personal being who talked with Suun and taught him kindly. At the first meeting, Suun heard sounds from the air, which were not heard by others, and trembled with such a great fear that his family thought that he was driven to madness (Choe 2009 [1881], 373-374). In Suun's experience, *hanalnim* was actively presiding over human history, though in Korea *hanalnim* was traditionally thought to be too high to come in direct contact with humans, like *deus otiosus* (Choi 2009b, 72). Jongseong Choi argues that the scene of the direct contact of *hanalnim* with Suun was surely influenced by Christian ideas because it did not appear in other Korean religious contexts before Suun (Choi 2009b, 30). Suun's *hanalnim* was the highest god who was transcendental and personal, and with whom human beings could and should be united (Jeong 2006, 219). It should be noted that God introduced himself as the highest god [上帝] and as a spirit also [鬼神]. According to Suun, the god identified himself as "the being human beings call *sangje*," the heavenly supreme god (Choe 2014 [1880], 14–15). Then the god identified himself as so-called a spirit (or a ghost) that human beings did not know (Choe 2014 [1880], 28). According to Suun's understanding, what people traditionally took as the

---

5. For further understanding of discussions on names of God in Donghak, see Im 2003, 129-132.

Korean Religious Texts in Iconic and Performative Rituals

Figure 7.3. "Jeopryeongganghwado," a print included in the *Sicheongyojoyujeokdoji* [A book of pictures and recordings of founders of Sicheongyo, a sect that branched off from Donghak] (1915). It depicts Suun's religious experience meeting God. He is bowing down to God who is not seen by others.

work of spirits was actually the result of God's actions (Choe 2009 [1881], 486). The god Suun believed he met was the highest being, who was at once intimately involved in big and small things of the world which Korean people thought of as the job of spirits.

In relation to Suun's notion of God, we can understand more easily "si-cheon-ju," which corresponds to the first three Chinese characters and three syllables in Korean recitation from the thirteen characters of Bonjumun. Sicheonju is the most important doctrine of Donghak, as a scholar of Donghak argues, "the experience of the incantation is the experience of sicheonju" (Kim 2013, 230). The main purpose of the incantation is sicheonju, which means serving God and having him abide in oneself. Anyone who recites the incantation was believed to serve God within oneself. The Korean verb *mosida* [모시다], which corresponds to the Chinese character *si* [侍], has many meanings, including "to serve," "to invite/take somebody in or to," or "to have someone be with one" (see Gukripgukeowon 2023). In the *Donggyeongdaejeon*, Suun himself interprets *si* as "having the divine spirit stay inside [a person, reciter], becoming assimilated with the divine energy outside, and everyone not straying from what one recognized" (Choe 2009 [1880], 94). To put it another way using Jongseong Choi's interpretation, members reciting the incantation aspired to invite and have God within themselves, to be united with God, and to reveal this union with God through their bodies, which were traditionally thought to be related to energy (Choi 2009b, 85-86). Furthermore, they repeatedly recited the incantation to serve and revere God, both during their everyday lives and during the rites for the worship of God (Choi 2009a, 163). This goal in reciting the incantation has been inherited by the contemporary Cheondogyo, whose members believe that they can focus their mind purely on God and be united with God by reciting the incantation (Yun and Hong 2016, 165-166). Donghak members recited the incantation to invite God inside, to be united with God, and to serve God, which was all integrated in the sound of si-cheon-ju and constituted the foremost purpose of the recitation.

Efficacy of reciting the incantation

While the incantation was thought to be an effective means to serve God, it was also believed to be invaluably helpful for people. The efficacy of reciting the incantation for people as shown in the scriptures can be summarized as follows.

First, the recitation of the incantation, which was called "the incantation study" or "the incantation training," was the most important way of cultivating themselves (Choi 2009b, 152-153). "The incantation took precedence over all others for religious practices of Donghak" (Yun 2014, 160). Early Donghak members tried to cultivate themselves by reciting the incantation (Choi 2009b, 151; Kim 2013, 239). It was the way they were able to become like Suun, reliving Suun's experience of meeting God and attaining a stage of maturity as high as Suun had achieved (Donghakhakhoe 2001, 42). In the *Donggyeongdaejeon*, Suun wrote that "the incantation is the letters for honoring God devotedly" (Choe 2009 [1880], 90). The phrase "honoring God" is often interpreted as "following God's will" (Yun and Hong 2016, 45). Based on this interpretation that the incantation is the letters that help people follow God's will, members can expect to cultivate themselves and become benevolent, righteous, courteous, and wise persons by reciting the incantation. More concretely speaking, the recitation was believed to make it possible for members to practice "*susimjeonggi*" [守 (or 修)心正氣], which Suun emphasized in both scriptures as practicing for self-cultivation (Choe 2009 [1880], 153; 2009 [1881], 497; see also Choe 2000 [1879], 78–79). *Susimjeonggi*, which literally means to maintain the mind and to straighten out the energy, can be understood as to practice maintaining the divine mind inside oneself and fulfilling God's will in daily life (Yun's annotation in Choe 2009 [1880], 154). Practicing *susimjeonggi* was believed to be possible by reciting the incantation (Yun and Hong 2016, 47).

Second, Suun argued that the incantation is effective for enabling people to live long and healthy lives. In the *Donggyeongdaejeon*, Suun described the scene of reciting the incantation as "[Donghak initiates] recited the incantation of long life, namely, the twenty-one characters" (Choe 2009 [1880], 149) making clear that the twenty-one-character incantation was effective for longevity. Another example is found in the early history book of Donghak. When the governor of the Gyeongsang province interrogated Suun and rebuked him for corrupting public morals, Suun stressed the efficaciousness of the incantation. He said that people were spontaneously cured without taking medicines when he taught them how to recite the incantation. He therefore denied that he was corrupting public morals (Choe 2000 [1879], 101).

Third, the incantation was said to be helpful for becoming intelligent and wise. As mentioned above, Suun asserts in the *Youngdamyusa* that if one recites the thirteen characters with utmost sincerity, he or she will become wise and not need any book of this world (Choe 2009 [1881], 358). The thirteen characters designate the Bonjumun, the second and main part of the twenty-one-character incantation. By reciting not even the twenty-one-character incantation, but just the second part of it, Suun argues, people can become so wise and bright that they will not need to get the knowledge from any other texts.

Fourth, it was believed that the incantation had the power to overwhelm devils and evil spirits. Suun wrote in "Gangsi," a short poem written in Chinese that is included in the *Donggyeongdaejeon*, "I wrote the twenty-one-character incantation and all the devils in the world surrendered" (Choe 2009 [1880], 211). Suun's successor Haewol included this poem in the early history of Donghak (Choe 2000 [1879], 267), which attests to early members' belief in the exorcising power of the incantation. It was Suun that received the incantation from God and wrote it in the form of language. All other Donghak members, all of whom were disciples of the Great Sacred Teacher Suun, had to do was to recite the incantation, which also had the power to make devils surrender.

In brief, the incantation was believed to be the text for serving God and for doing good for people. Reciting the incantation was an efficacious ritual performance of Donghak. The incantation is still the first among the five basic rituals of contemporary Cheondogyo, and is always involved in the other four rituals and regarded as the most effective way to fulfill God's will (Yun and Hong 2016, 49, 154; Choi and Park 2020, 62). The incantation as the text of heaven could be ritualized most easily by performing the recitation. The proper requirements of this ritualization will be explained in the next section.

Proper recitation of the incantation:
Reciting sincerely in thinking significance

The incantation should be recited properly for the reciter to obtain its effects such as assimilation with God, cultivating himself or herself, becoming wise, and living a long and healthy life. First, the incantation should be taught correctly and recited exactly. Suun pointed out that it was wrong and shameful for some people not to learn the incantation properly but to repeat incorrect phrases that they heard by chance from others (Choe 2009 [1880], 159). The incantation had to be handed down exactly from a qualified member of Donghak to the learner. To convey a wrong version of the incantation was regarded as "violating the sacred virtues" of the incantation (Choe 2000 [1879], 89).

Second, the incantation should be recited sincerely, with all one's heart. As mentioned above, Suun wrote in the *Yongdamyusa* that the incantation should be recited with utmost sincerity; the reciter should focus on the recitation itself and think about God alone. In addition, it had to be recited with good posture and modest attitude. In the *Donggyeongdaejwon*, when Suun wrote about appropriate behaviors that Donghak members should conduct, he mainly mentioned morally sound activities or attitudes, such as being dressed decently, not eating while walking on the street, not assuming a haughty attitude, and not eating dog meat. He emphasized only one rule about religious activity, which was related to the proper way of reciting the incantation. He said that Donghak members should not recite in a loud voice while lying down because it was not a sign of sincerity, but of negligence (Choe 2009 [1880], 153). The reciters should show their respect and true heart by assuming a humble and courteous attitude.

Third, though the incantation should be recited as frequently and constantly as possible, it should not be repeated mechanically. There are heroic stories of early leaders of Donghak that stress their hard training of repeating the incantation. Haewol said that their study and training were made possible only by reciting the incantation. And he himself endeavored to recite it as much as possible. When training with two other members in Jeokjoam temple in Taebaek Mountain, he recited the incantation, fingering prayer beads, twenty- to thirty-thousand times every day for forty-nine training days (Choe 2000, 215–216; Choi and Park 2020, 143). Byeonghui Son, who was designated by Haewol as the third leader, is reported to have recited the incantation thirty thousand times to train himself every day for three years after he converted to Donghak (Yun and Hong 2016, 68). Son's replacement and fourth leader of Cheondogyo, Inho Pak, is said to have recited the incantation day and night for ten years. He kept reciting during his waking hours. When he slept, he put his head on a sickle handle instead of a pillow, trying not to fall fast asleep and began to recite right after he woke up (Yun and Hong 2016, 71).

Finally, the proper recitation should involve the appropriate understanding of the content of the incantation. As seen above, it was Suun himself who provided detailed interpretation of the incantation in *Donggyeongdaejeon*. From the beginning of Donghak, the semantic dimension of the incantation, so-called the text of heaven, was regarded as significant along with its performance by the recitation. However, it should be noted that though elite members could ritualize the performative dimension and the semantic dimension of the incantation at the same time while reciting it, the general public could not. Suun may not have expected the public, who constituted most of the early members, to fully understand what they recited or to know its philosophical and theological interpretation. Suun's elaborate exposition of the incantation in the *Donggyeondaejeon* was surely meant for intellectuals. In this scripture, as I wrote above, Suun provides the detailed explanation of the incantation to "wise (or virtuous) [Confucian] scholars" [賢士] who visited Suun to learn about his teaching. These wise scholars among the members were able to contemplate its meaning while reciting it. But he did not explain its content in the Korean-language *Yongdamyusa*, but emphasized its importance and efficacy instead. In addition, it must not have been easy for members to think about its content while they repeatedly recited it many times. It is one thing to recite it with sincerity and another to do it while thinking about the content. Early leaders' heroic training of reciting thirty thousand times a day hardly seems to ritualize its semantic dimension.

However, in early Donghak, we can find the idea that both the semantic dimension and the performative dimension should be ritualized together in order to distinguish it readily as divine words and to appropriate it. Haewol thought that all members should not give up knowing the substance of the incantation as well as reciting it (Choe 2000 [1879], 135). Haewol was younger than Suun by just three years but was his most enthusiastic, faithful, and trusted disciple. After Suun's death, he took charge of repairing the weakened organization and establishing it as a religious institution. Unlike Suun who was educated in classical Chinese in youth, Haewol had to do manual labor without obtaining a proper education due to poverty, but he learned from Suun in person and kept applying himself to studying what Suun taught. He successfully developed his own interpretation of the two scriptures including the incantation and tried to explain it to the public. He asserted that performing the recitation and knowing the contents should not be separated while he himself recited the incantation constantly. Haewol said,

> It is not right to only recite the incantation without thinking about its logic and significance, while it is also not right to try to only study its logic and significance without performing its recitation. Members must be perfect at both [performing the recitation and learning the significance].
>
> (Quoted from Yun and Hong 2016, 169)

It is obvious that Haewol pursued both the semantic and performative dimensions of the incantation. Though Haewol was not from the intellectual elite, he was not only well versed in what Suun taught, but also developed his own interpretation. He expounded important phrases of the two scriptures including the incantation, such as the ideas of having God inside, serving God, and being united with God. He believed that the public could learn the content of the scriptures just as he did.

To recite the incantation properly, members were supposed to focus on God and concentrate on recitation. It should be repeated constantly with utmost sincerity to have the power of divine words exercised, for instance, to subdue devils, to cultivate oneself, and to become wise and bright to the level of not needing any other books. While it would be difficult to contemplate its contents while reciting the incantation composed in Chinese, early members thought that even the public should be good at both learning the contents and performing the recitation. In early Donghak, we find the idea that a religious text can be more efficiently ritualized when the performative dimension works together with the semantic dimension even if it is composed in a foreign language unknown to most members.

Yongdamyusa made for being recited

Until now, this chapter has focused on reciting the incantation, which was included in the *Donggyeongdaejeon* and regarded as "the text of heaven" itself. Though all Donghak members should and could recite the incantation, most of them could not memorize or recite the whole *Donggyeongdaejeon* written in Chinese. Many of them did recite pieces in the *Yongdamyusa*, which were written in Korean verse. As I wrote above, *Yongdamyusa* was composed of eight lengthy pieces of *gasa*, a traditional Korean literature genre that is often placed in between poetry and prose. Suun wrote *gasa* pieces included in the *Yongdamyusa* in Korean in order to propagate the sect to common people who had no knowledge of classical Chinese. We can clearly see that the *Yongdamyusa* was made for the general public in its designation of the incantation. As I wrote above, it is only in "Gyonhunga" and "Heungbiga" of the *Yongdamyusa* that Suun referred to the incantation not as twenty-one characters, but as thirteen characters, which corresponds to the Bonjumun part (Choe 2009 [1881], 358, 504). Suun seemed intent on mitigating the burden for non-elite members who could not read or write Chinese characters by lessening the number of characters to memorize.

In the *Yongdamyusa*, Suun declared the purpose of the new religion, explained its basic doctrines, encouraged his followers to cultivate themselves, and also described his deep impressions of the revelations that he received from God. If we summarize the contents of the *Yongdamyusa*, aside from some stories and sermons, the book was a scripture made for recitation since *gasa* were supposed to be recited. Suun wrote *gasa* that later became chapters of the *Yongdamyusa*. They spread among members by way of recitation. In practice, *gasa* works included in the *Yongdamyusa* were always recited by members, with cadences and often to simple tunes.

For readers who do not know about the *gasa* genre, I would like to insert a brief explanation here. *Gasa* is a Korean traditional poetry genre, which most scholars agree were first composed by Hyegeun, a Buddhist monk also called Naong (1320-1376), to inculcate Buddhist teachings for the public in the late Goryeo Dynasty, of which the national religion was Buddhism. Before *Hangeul*, the Korean alphabet, was made in 1443 and promulgated in 1446 by King Sejong of the Joseon Dynasty, *gasa* was recited in Korean but written by using the sounds and meanings of Chinese letters. This genre became popular starting in the fifteenth century and famous pieces were written by Confucian scholars in Korean in the sixteenth century. From the late eighteenth century many *gasa* works were made by commoners who tried to portray their ideas and sentiments in them. Many religious *gasa* works were produced, mainly for the purpose of mass propagation,

Scriptures for Recitation in Donghak

in the nineteenth century and the early twentieth century by Catholics, Buddhists, and members of new religious movements including Donghak (Donghakhakhoe 2001, 68–69; Park 2021, 4–21).

Gasa could be conveyed to the public, including women and children, and was relatively easily understood and memorized because it was written in colloquial Korean and had rhythm (Park 2021, 194). Gasa has meter, known in Korean as "*eumbo*," which corresponds to foot in English poetry. It designates a unit of reading without pause and corresponds to the length of time for reading a word segment. A line of gasa consists of four segments, and is called "*saeumbo* (four *eumbo*)." Here is a phonetic transliteration of a line from "Gyohunga" in the *Yongdamyusa*: "*ggumilreonga jamilreonga mugeukdaedo badanaeya.*" It has four segments of words, each of which has four syllables, which will be recited as "*ggu-mil-reon-ga* (very brief pause) *ja-mil-reon-ga* (very brief pause) *mu-geuk-dae-do* (very brief pause) *ba-da-nae-ya* (brief pause then next line)." The person who created or learned a gasa piece would recite it in the cadence of four *eumbo* and to a simple tune that he or she improvised. When a person recited gasa, people around him or her could join in. Readers who have seen a squad or platoon of soldiers in the army run together would be able to imagine how Korean people recited a gasa piece. It is not sung like a song, but it is recited to some rhythm and tune. Though gasa is poetry, it often contains elements commonly found in prose writings, such as a long story or moral teachings, because its length is not limited. Therefore, Byoung Hoon Park translates gasa as "prose-poetry" (Park 2021, 193).

Early Donghak members were not only encouraged to recite gasa pieces from the *Yongdamyusa* but also liked to recite them. Suun created his gasa works to have them recited in cadence and tune, which made it easier for members to memorize them. In the last two lines of "Dodeokga" in the *Yongdamyusa*, Suun wrote, "Cultivate right mind by reciting exactly (or memorizing) a few phrases of gasa composed in Korean just as you hear them, and then do not forget and think about it" (Choe 2009 [1881], 498). Suun is making it clear in this part that he made gasa pieces for members to memorize and recite (Cho, 1991). They resemble recited scriptures of other religious traditions that also tend "to use tone and rhythm to project the voice and make the reading more memorable" (Watts 2017, 259).

The *Yongdamyusa* was not only spread orally, but also published as woodblock printed books in 1881, 1891, and 1922. Haewol and other leaders were concerned that the original works of Suun might be changed and stained if they were transmitted orally alone (see Cho, 1991). But these publications did not result in giving up the recitation. On the contrary, the published books were helpful for members to recite the exact words of Suun. It was important for members to recite the same words the Great Sacred Teacher made and recited, following the rhythm he created in order to repeat his own words and to relive his experiences through their mouths.

Suun unfolded his ideas and experiences mostly with enthusiasm and feeling, but sometimes showed his imperturbable calmness in verse pieces of the *Yongdamyusa*. I select conspicuous themes which Suun deployed throughout the scripture, without distinguishing the chapters, as follows: the deplorable situation of the times in which people lived selfish lives without understanding God's will; the story of Suun receiving the endless great way from God who chose him though there were many people better than him; his work of disseminating the twenty-one character incantation; the expectation that Donghak would make people better and change the world; the importance of revering God even while eating meals; the identification of his teaching as Eastern Learning that should be strictly distinguished from Western Learning (Catholicism); criticisms of Catholic doctrines such as faith in heaven and disapproval of ancestral rites; the view of humans as the most spiritual (or sacred) beings among the creatures of the world, but futile also without the mind of revering God; the hardships, like slanders and false charges, which he had to face while spreading Donghak teachings; encouragement to his disciples to cultivate themselves, especially by reciting the incantation, even under persecution.

Two remarkable features of the *Yongdamyusa* were helpful for gaining public support. First, Suun talked candidly about his personal experiences and emotions, such as looking back on his wandering around from place to place when he was younger; having enjoyable talks with his wife; his pride in his hometown as a propitious site; his deep regret over failing to fulfil his filial duty; and the fact that his family members were perplexed at his mysterious experience of meeting God because they thought he was suffering from mental illness. Suun's personal emotions and experiences contained in the scripture made its listeners and readers feel closer and more sympathetic to him. Second, many parts in the *Yongdamyusa* reflected ideas and practices that prevailed among the people already, such as geomancy and prophecy. For instance, Suun implied that he could be chosen by God as his messenger because his hometown was an auspicious site, foretelling his fortune would last fifty thousand years (Choe 2009 [1881], 408). Besides, he promised people that they would be blessed in this world if they accepted Donghak. For instance, he argued that unidentified epidemics, like what had been prevalent in Korea for three years, would not break out if people would revere God following the way of Donghak (Choe 2009 [1881], 476).

The original reason Suun wrote the Korean *gasa* pieces later collected in the *Yongdamyusa* was surely to edify the public more easily, while doctrines developed in the Chinese *Donggyeongdaejeon*, whose target readers were "wise scholars," were based on Confucian views (Donghakhakhoe 2009, 56). To achieve his popularizing goal, Suun used tones that are admonitory, persuasive, and often repetitive, similar to other religious *gasa* pieces of the time (Donghakhakhoe 2009, 67–71). In addition to educating people, this Korean scripture was intended to allow the general public to memorize and recite it easily. Some of the public members of Donghak, including women and people of lower classes, could read Korean written language used in the published book of the *Yongdamyusa*, though they did not know classical Chinese. More people who were illiterate even in Korean had no choice but to learn by listening and participate in reciting by singing works to a rhythm. Many of them could memorize all the chapters of the scripture by listening to them being recited and in turn by reciting them over and over.

To sum up, the *Yongdamyusa* was made for the two purposes of edification and recitation, which could be fulfilled because it was composed in Korean verse. The chapters in the *Yongdamyusa* could be easily understood because they were composed in Korean that most people used in daily conversation. While Suun systematized his thoughts in the *Donggyeongdaejeon* persuasively to the intellectuals, it was difficult to represent and appeal to Korean sentiments by using Chinese. The *Yongdamyusa* played the role of "the source of Donghak teachings for the public," helping them to understand and accept the newly developed thoughts and practices of Donghak (Donghakhakhoe 2001, 51–53). In addition, members could easily memorize and recite them first and foremost because they were verse works that had cadence and tune. The *Yongdamyusa* was an effective tool of performance. By reciting it, members could say the exact words the Great Sacred Teacher uttered to the rhythm he developed, and so they could reproduce and relive his teaching and life. The semantic and performative dimensions of the scripture could be simultaneously ritualized in the recitation of the *Yongdamyusa*.

Explained in scriptures and reciting scriptures

This chapter has illuminated how the two sacred texts of Donghak, the twenty-one-character incantation and the *Yongdamyusa*, were ritualized. In the two canonical scriptures of Donghak, the *Donggyeongdaejeon* and the *Yongdamyusa*, Suun explained how and what he received from God, which are equivalent to the origin and the core idea of *Donghak*. It was believed that both the origin and the core idea were summarized in the twenty-one-character incantation. The incantation is the core scripture called "the text of heaven," which is included, explained, and emphasized in the scriptures. These sacred words given to Suun directly by God were at the center of all the teachings and rituals of Donghak. The performance of reciting the incantation was the most desirable and effective way of serving and being united with God. Most members could not read the *Donggyeongdaejeon* written in classical Chinese and it was therefore not possible for them to memorize and recite the whole book. But the incantation, a brief part of it, could and should be recited. The power of the sacred text was based on its acceptance as divine words by Donghak members and it could be exercised through performing its recitation repeatedly and devoutly. Reciting should be repeated constantly and early Donghak leaders recited it up to thirty thousand times a day. Contemporary Cheondogyo members still recite the incantation as an independent ritual performance during all the other major rituals, and as well as in their everyday lives. Simultaneously, as Haewol, the successor of Suun, emphasized, members should learn and study its logic and meaning along with its recitation. Haewol had members of the public familiarize themselves with its contents through constant education. Recitation conjoined with understanding was thought to be proper and more efficacious.

The recitation of the *Yongdamyusa* was deeply rooted in the lives of early Donghak members, though it was not used in rituals like the incantation. While the whole book or each chapter of the *Donggyeongdaejeon* that was written in classical Chinese was very difficult for general members to recite, the *Yongdamyusa* written in a Korean verse genre, *gasa*, was created to be recited and was spread by the recitation. Members enjoyed learning and reciting chapters in the *Yongdamyusa*, which were composed in easily understandable Korean verse to be recited to rhythm and tune. Members could repeat Suun's experience of being united with God through reciting Suun's own testimonies. The *Yongdamyusa* provides a vivid example of how the genre of scripture can be critical for its ritualization. The recitation of scripture can be performed more efficiently when reciters can use rhythm and tune while fully understanding the contents.

In the recitation of Donghak scriptures, we can see that the semantic dimension of the text extends to the non-intellectual public for its efficient ritualization. The more popular Korean scripture *Yongdamyusa* was intended to be studied and simultaneously performed in the sense that it was made to be recited in colloquial Korean and in verse. In the case of the *Donggyeongdaejeon*, the scripture written in Chinese but used in Korea, only a minority of members who commanded the scholarly language of Chinese could ritualize the semantic and the performative dimensions simultaneously. Yet by reciting the doubly-ritualized incantation, that is, by differentiating again a very brief part of the *Donggyeongdaejeon*, which itself was a differentiated text, as the words directly from God and the text of heaven, most members of the public could possibly ritualize two dimensions of the text. When members combined the performance of reciting the incantation with the study of its semantic dimension, they could achieve the goal of serving and being united with God, as well as appropriating the divine power in their lives.

Bibliography

An, Sanggyeong. 2009. *Anjeungut Mugyeong* [shamanic scriptures for sitting rites]. Seoul: Minsokwon.
———. 2010a. "Chungcheong-do Anjeungut Jikyeo-on Gono Gyeonggaeng-ui Hanseureon Chugwon" [prayers with deep sorrow of the lonely shaman reciting scriptures who has maintained the traditional sitting rites of the Chuncheong provinces]. *Minjok21* 2010(5): 146–151.
———. 2010b. "Gyeryongsan Samsindanggut Mugyeong-ui Gujo-wa Uimi" [Structure and meaning of shamanic scriptures for the samsindang rites in the area of the Gyeryong mountain]. *Urimalgeul: The Korean Language and Literature* 50: 129–159.
Austin, John L. 1962. *How to do Things with Words*. Cambridge, MA: Harvard University Press, (Reprinted 1975).
Bell, Catherine. 1992. *Ritual Theory, Ritual Practice*. Oxford: Oxford University Press.
———. 1997. *Ritual: Perspectives and Dimensions*. Oxford: Oxford University Press.
"Bokjang." 2010. In *Doopedia Dusanbaekgoa* (Dusan Encyclopedia). Available at: http://www.doopedia.co.kr/doopedia/master/master.do?_method=view&MAS_IDX=101013000870987. Accessed July 15, 2017.
Brown, C. Mackenzie. 1986. "Purāna as Scripture: From Sound to Image of the Holy Word in the Hindu Tradition." *History of Religions* 26(1): 68–86.
"Buheungsagyeonghoe-wa Gyohoe" [The revival Bible study meeting and church]. 2006. An Editorial of *Hankook Jangro Sinmun*. 18/3/2006.
Cabezón, José Ignacio. 2004. "Scripture." In *Encyclopedia of Buddhism*, vol. 2, edited by Robert E. Buswell Jr., 755–758. New York: Thomson Gale.
Ching, Julia. 2000. *The Religious Thought of Chu Hsi*. Oxford: Oxford University Press.
Cho, Dongil. 1991. "Donghak Gasa." In *Hangukminjokmunhwadaebaekguasajeon* [Encyclopedia of Korean Culture], Seongnam: The Academy of Korean Studies. https://encykorea.aks.ac.kr/Article/E0016858. 10/3/2023.
Cho, Hyeonbum. 2018. "Yunjichung-ui pyejebunju nongeo-e daehan il gochal [A study on the seasons of ancestor worship refusal of Yoon Ji Choong]." *Jonggyoyeongu* 78(1): 141–174.

Choe, Je-u. 2009 [1880, 1881]. *Juhae Donghakgyeongjeon: Donggyeongdaejeon/ Yongdamyusa* [Annotated scriptures of dongahak]. Translated and annotated by Seoksan Yun. Seoul: Donghaksa.

———. 2014 [1880]. *Donggyeongdaejeon*. Translated from Classical Chinese into Korean and Annotated by Seoksan Yun. Seoul: Mosineunsaramdeul.

Choe, Sihyeong. 2000 [1879]. *Chogi Donahak-ui Yeoksa: Dowongiseo* [A history of early donghak]. Translated from Classical Chinese into Korean and annotated by Seoksan Yun. Seoul: Sinseowon.

Choi, Geunyeong. 1996. "Gagugyeonghaeng." In *Pascal Dongsuh's Korea-World Encyclopedia* vol. 1, 29. Seoul: Dongsuhmunhwa publishing.

Choi, Jongseong. 2009a. "Chogi Donghak-ui Sinhak-gwa Uiryehak: Cheonje-wa Susimjeongki" [Theology and rituals of Early Donghak: Ritual to heavenly gods and susimjeongki (keeping the good mind and having the right force)]. *Hankukmunhwa* 45: 159–176.

———. 2009b. *Donghak-ui Theopraxy: Chogi Donghak mit Hugi Donghak-ui Sasang-gwa Uirye* [Theopraxy of donghak: Thoughts and rituals of early donghak and later donghak]. Seoul: Minsokwon.

Choi, Jongseong and Byoung Hoon Park. 2020. *Sicheongyoyujeokdoji: Geurim-euro Ikneun tto dareun Dongahanksa* [Pictures with explanations on the history of founding fathers of Sicheongyo: Another history of Donghak read by pictures]. Seoul: Mosineunsaramdeul.

Chu, Hsi. 1977. *Chu-tzu yü-lei* [朱子語類, *Classified Conversations of Master Chu*]. Edited by Li Jingde in 1473. Seoul: a Facsimile edition (Seoul National University Library, 181. 1346 J868ef).

Clark, A. D. 1930. *The Korean Church and the Nevius Methods*. New York: Fleming H. Revell.

Confucius. 2003. *Lúnyǔ* (論語, *Analects*). Translated into Korean and Annotated by Gangsu Lee *et al.* Seoul: Jisiksaneopsa, published in Classical Chinese and Korean.

Dallapiccola, A. L. 2004. "Stupa." In *Encyclopedia of Buddhism*, vol. 2, edited by Robert E. Buswell Jr., 803–808. New York: Thomson Gale.

De Simini, Florinda. 2016. *Of Gods and Books: Ritual and Knowledge Transmission in the Manuscript Cultures of Premodern India*. Berlin: De Gruyter.

Deuchler, Martina. 1992. *The Confucian Transformation of Korea: A Study of Society and Ideology*. Cambridge, MA: Council on East Asian Studies, Harvard University.

Donghakhakhoe [The Association of Donkank Studies]. 2001. *Donghak-gwa Donghakgyeongjeon-ui Jaeinsik* [Reconsidering donghank and donghak scriptures]. Seoul: Sinseowon.

Doniger, Wendy. 1998. *The Implied Spider: Politics & Theology in Myth*. New York: Columbia University Press.

———. 1999. *Splitting the Difference: Gender and Myth in Ancient Greece and India*. Chicago, IL: University of Chicago Press.

———. 2000. "Post-Modern and Colonial Structural Comparisons." In *A Magic Still Dwells: Comparative Religion in the Postmodern Age*, edited by K. C. Patton and B. C. Ray, 63–74. Berkeley: University of California Press.
Dupré, Louis. 2000. *Symbols of the Sacred*. Grand Rapids, MI: Eerdmans Publishing.
Eliade, Mircea. 1949. *Patterns in Comparative Religion*. Trans. by Rosemary Sheed. New York: Sheed and Ward (reprinted 1958).
———. 1957. *The Sacred and the Profane: the Nature of Religion*. New York: Harcourt (reprinted 1987).
———. 1960 [1957]. *Myths, Dreams and Mysteries*. Translated by Philip Mairet. New York: Harper & Row.
———. 1982 [1978]. *Ordeal by Labyrinth: Conversations with Claude-Henri Rocquet*. Translated by Derek Coltman. Chicago, IL: University of Chicago Press.
Esposito, John L., Darrell J. Fasching, and Todd T. Lewis. 2015. *World Religions Today* (5th edition). Oxford: Oxford University Press.
"Gagugyeonghaeng." 1983. *Donga World Encyclopedia*, vol. 1, 37. Seoul: Donga.
Gardner, Daniel K. 2004. "Attentiveness and Meditative Reading in Cheng-Zhu Neo-Confucianism." In *Confucian Spirituality*, vol. 2, edited by Tu Weiming and Mary Evelyn Tucker, 99–119. New York: The Crossroad Publishing.
Geertz, Clifford. 1973. *The Interpretation of Cultures*. New York: Basic Books.
Gethin, Rupert. 1998. *The Foundations of Buddhism*. Oxford: Oxford University Press.
Geum, Jangtae. 2001. Seonghaksipttowa T'oegye Cheolhagui Gujo [Seonghaksiptto and the Structure in the Philosophy of T'oegye]. Seoul: Seoul National University Press.
———. 2013. T'oegye Pyeongjeon [*Critical Biography of T'oegye*]. Seoul: Jisikgwagyoyang.
Gidoksinbo [Christian messenger Newspaper] 1916–1918. Seoul.
Geurisdosinmun [Christ Newspaper]. 1898–1902. Seoul.
Gojongsillok book 1. 20, December, 1863. *The Veritable Records of Joseon Dynasty* (history.go.kr).
Gombrich, Richard. 1990. "How the Mahayana Began." In *The Buddhist Forum, Volume 1: Seminar Papers 1987-1988*, edited by Tadeusz Skorupski, 21–30. London: School of Oriental and African Studies, University of London.
Graham, William A. 1987. *Beyond the Written Word: Oral Aspects of Scripture in the History of Religion*. Cambridge: Cambridge University Press.
———. 1989. "Scripture as Spoken Word." In *Rethinking Scripture: Essays from a Comparative Perspective*, edited by Miriam Levering, 129–169. Albany: State University of New York Press.
Gregory, Peter N., ed. 1986. *Traditions of Meditation in Chinese Buddhism*. Honolulu: University of Hawaii Press.
Gu, Junghoe. 2001. Gyeryongsan Gutdang Yeongu [A study of the hall of shamanic rites in the area of the Gyeryong mountain]. Seoul: Gukhakjaryowon.
———. 2009. Gyeongchaek Munhwa-wa Yeoksa [Culture and history of shamanic scriptures]. Seoul: Minsokwon.

Gukripgukeowon [National Institute of Korean Language]. 2023. Pyonjugukeodaesajeon [Standard Dictionary of Korean Language], https://stdict.korean.go.kr/main/main.do.

Hangukgidokgyoyeoksayeonguso [Institute for Korean church history]. 1989, 1990. *Hangukgidokgyouiyeoksa I, II* [A history of Korean church I, II]. Seoul: Gidokgyomunsa.

Han, Jeongdeok. 2017. "Seolwi-seolgyeong-gwa Gyeongjeon" [*seolwi-seolgyeong* and shamanic scriptures] Interview with Yohan Yoo conducted on May 18.

Harari, Yuval Noah. 2015 [2011]. *Sapiens: A Brief History of Humankind*. London: Vintage.

Harvey, B. Peter. 1990. *An Introduction to Buddhism: Teachings, History, and Practices*. New York: Cambridge University Press.

Hennessey, Anna Madelyn. 2011. "Chinese Images of Body and Landscape: Visualization and Representation in the Religious Experience of Medieval China." Ph.D. Dissertation, UC Santa Barbara.

Hong, Hangpyo. 1999. "A Study on the Impact of Bible Study Meetings of Great Spiritual Awakening on the Development of Spirituality." Unpublished PhD Thesis, Ashland Theological Seminary.

Im, Seungbeom. 2009. "Chungcheonggut-ui Seolgyeong Yeon-gu" [A study on *seolgyeong* of shamanic rites in Chuncheong area] *Korean Shamanism* 18: 83–107.

———. 2011. *Taean Seolwi-seolgyeong*. Seoul: Minsokwon.

Im, Taehong. 2003. "Donghak-ui Seonglipgwajeong-e Michin Yuhak-ui Yeonghyang" [Influence of Confucianism on the establishment of Donghak]. *Sinjonggyoyeongu* 9: 115–144.

Jang, Inseong. 2013. "Chungcheong Jiyeok-ui Anjeungut-gwa Jeongilgyo" [sitting rites of Chuncheong area and Jeongilgyo] *The Journal of Humanities Studies* 93: 341–360.

Jay, Nancy. 1992. *Throughout Your Generations Forever: Sacrifice, Religion, and Paternity*. Chicago, IL: University of Chicago Press.

Jeong, Hyejeong. 2006. "Donghak uirye-wa 'Susimjeongki' Suhaeng-ui Yu-bul-jeok Ihae" [The ceremony of Donghak and Confucian/Buddhist understanding of 'susimjeongki']. *Hankuksasang-gwa munhwa* 34: 217–243.

Jeong, Sunu. 2007. *Gongbuui Balgyeon* [Discovery of Study]. Seoul: Hyeonamsa.

Jeontongbulbokjang mit jeomanuisikbojonhoe [Jeontongbulbokjang]. 2014. *Jeontong Bulbokjanguisik Mit Jeomanuisik* [Traditional rites of storing sacred objects in Buddha statues and of drawing eyes on them]. Seoul: Bulgyomunhwajaeyeonguso.

Jones, Lindsay, ed. 2005. *Encyclopedia of Religion*, 2nd edition, vol. 14. Farmington Hills, MI: Thompson Gale.

Ju, Gyeong-mi. 2004. "Hanguk Bulsarijangeom-e Iseoseo *Mugujeongguangdaedaranigyeong*-ui Uiui" [The significance of *Rasmivimalavisuddhaprabhanama-dharani-sutra* in Korean Buddhist reliquaries]. *Journal of Buddhist Art* 2: 164–196.

———. 2016. "Silla Jungdae Bulsarijangeom-ui Dayangseong-gua Munhwasajeok Uiui" [Stylistic multiplicity of Buddhist reliquaries in the middle Silla dynasty and its cultural and historical meaning]. *Sogang Journal of Early Korean History* 23: 249–290.
Kalton, Michael C. 1988. *To Become a Sage: The Ten Diagrams on Sage Learning by Yi T'oegye*. New York: Columbia University Press.
Kim, Gwangsu. 1996. "Sagyeonghoe, Hangukgyohoe" [The Bible study meeting, Korean church]. In *The Encyclopedia of Christianity*, Gidokgyomunsa, vol. 4, 292–293. Seoul: Kidok-Kyomunsa.
Kim, Insu. 2002. *Hanguk Gidokgyohoe-ui Yeoksa I* [The history of Korean Christian church I]. Seoul: Presbyterian Seminary Press.
Kim, Yeongjin, Hyejeong Park and Sanggyeong An. 2012. *Chungcheong-do Anjeungut* [sitting rites of Chuncheong provinces]. Cheongju: Chungcheongbuk-do Munhwa Yusan Yeon-guhoe.
Kim, Yonghwi. 2013. "Donghak-ui Sudo-wa Jumunsuryeon-ui Uimi" [Meaning of ascetic training and incantation training in Donghak]. *Seondomunhwa* 14: 219–252.
Kinnard, Jacob N. 2002. "On Buddhist 'Bibliolaters': Representing and Worshiping the Book in Medieval Indian Buddhism." *The Eastern Buddhist* 34: 94–116.
Korean Statistical Information Service (KOSIS). 2007 (1930). https://kosis.kr/statHtml/statHtml.do?orgId=101&tblId=DT_1IN3015&conn_path=I2.
Kugel, James L. 1997. *The Bible as It Was*. Cambridge, MA: Belknap.
Küng, Hans and Julia Ching. 1989. *Christianity and Chinese Religions*. New York: Doubleday.
Levering, Miriam. 1989. "Scripture and Its Reception: A Buddhist Case." In *Rethinking Scripture: Essays from a Comparative Perspective*, ed. Miriam Levering, 58–101. Albany: State University of New York Press.
Li Ji (禮記, *Book of Rites*). 1985. Translated into Korean and Annotated by Sangok Lee. Seoul: Myeongmundang, published in Classical Chinese and Korean.
Lofton, Kathryn. 2017. *Consuming Religion*. Chicago, IL: University of Chicago Press.
McMahan, David L. 2010. "Vision and Visualization." http://www.oxfordbibliographies.com. Accessed on 1/7/2015. DOI: 10.1093/obo/9780195393521-0175
Meyer, Birgit, David Morgan, Crispin Paine and S. Brent Plate. 2011. "Introduction: Key Words in Material Religion." *Material Religion* 7(1): 4–9.
Min, Gyungbae. 1993. *Hangukgidokgyohoesa* [Korean Christian church history]. Seoul: Yonsei University Press.
Mitchell, Donald W. 2002. *Buddhism: Introducing the Buddhist Experience*. Oxford: Oxford University Press.
Moerman, D. Max. 2010. "The Death of the Dharma: Buddhist Sutra Burials in Early Medieval Japan." In *The Death of Sacred Texts: Ritual Disposal and Renovations of Texts in World Religions*, edited by Kristina Myrvold, 71–90. Farnham: Ashgate.

Moffett, Samuel Hugh. 1962. *The Christians of Korea*. New York: Friendship Press.
Moore, J. Z. 1907. "The Great Revival Year." *The Korean Mission Field* (August).
Moore, S. F. 1906. "The Revival in Seoul." *The Korean Mission Field* (April).
Morgan, David. 2005. *The Sacred Gaze: Religious Visual Culture in Theory and Practice*. Berkeley: University of California Press.
Mun, Myeongdae. 1991. "Bokjang." In *Hanguk Minjok Munhwa Daebaekgua* [*Encyclopedia of Korean Culture*]. http://encykorea.aks.ac.kr/Contents/Index. Accessed July 3, 2017.
Oh, Munseon. 1997. "Buyeo Jiyeok-ui Anjeungut" [sitting rites in Buyeo area] *The Journal of Korean Historical-folklife* 6: 91–121.
———. 2016. "Beopsa." In *Han-guk Minsok Daebaekgwa Sajeon* [*Encyclopedia of Korean Folk Culture*]. Internet edition. http://folkency.nfm.go.kr/kr/topic/%EB%B2%95%EC%82%AC/2168. Accessed 30 August 2017.
Orsi, Robert A. 2016. *History and Presence*. Cambridge, MA: Harvard University Press.
Park, Byoung Hoon. 2021. "A Study on Prose-Poetry of New Religions in Modern Korea: Focusing on the Relationship between Fate of the Period and Morality." Unpublished Ph.D. thesis, Seoul National University.
Park, Hyejeong. 2014. *Yangban Go-eul Yangban Gut: Chungnam-ui Anjeungut Eumak* [Shamanic rituals of noblemen in the village of noblemen: music of sitting rites in the South Chunchoeng Province]. Seoul: Minsokwon.
Park, Jeongho. 2017. "Silsangsa Bulsang Meori-eseo Saero Chajeun Bulgyeong" [A Buddhist Sutra Found in the Head of a Buddha Statue in Silsangsa Temple]. *Joonangilbo*, May 24. Available at: https://www.joongang.co.kr/article/21602102#home. Accessed March 4, 2023.
Park, Jong-ik. 2010. "Daejeon Anjeungut Munyeo Songseonja-ui Gyebo-wa Seolgyeong" [genealogy and *seolgyeong* of Song Seonja, a female shaman performing sitting rites in the area of Daejeon] *The Journal of Humanities Studies* 79: 63–88.
Parmenter, Dorina Miller. 2012 [2017]. "How the Bible Feels: The Christian Bible as Effective and Affective Object." *Postscripts* 8(1–2): 27–37. [Reprinted in *Sensing Sacred Texts*, edited by James W. Watts, 27–37. Sheffield: Equinox, 2018].
Patton, C. Kimberley. 2009. *Religion of the Gods: Ritual, Paradox, and Reflexivity*. Oxford: Oxford University Press.
Peters, F. E. 2007. *The Voice, the Word, the Books: The Sacred Scriptures of the Jews, Christians, and Muslims*. Princeton, NJ: Princeton University Press.
Plate, Brent S. 2014. *A History of Religion in 5 1/2 Objects: Bringing the Spiritual to its Senses*. Boston, MA: Beacon Press.
Rappaport, Roy A. 1999. *Ritual and Religion in the Making of Humanity*. Cambridge: Cambridge University Press.
Ray, Benjamin Caleb. 2000. "Discourse about Difference: Understanding African Ritual Language." In *A Magic Still Dwells: Comparative Religion in the Postmodern Age*, edited by Kimberley C. Patton and Benjamin C. Ray, 101–116. Berkeley: University of California Press.

Bibliography

Rhi, Juhyung. 2004. "Gandhara Bulsang-gwa Sari Bongan" [The installation of a relic in Buddha image of Gandhara]. *Central Asian Studies* 9: 129–159.
Ricoeur, Paul. 1976. *Interpretation Theory: Discourse and Surplus of Meaning*. Texas: Texas Christian University Press.
———. 1995. *Figuring the Sacred: Religion, Narrative, and Imagination*. Minneapolis, MN: Fortress Press.
Robinson, Richard H. and Willard L. Johnson. 1997. *The Buddhist Religion: A Historical Introduction*. 4th ed. Belmont: Wadsworth Publishing Company.
Saemunangyohoechulpanbu [Publishing Department in Saemunan Church]. 1958. *Saemunangyohoe Chilsipnyeonsa* [The History of 70 years of Saemunan Church]. Seoul: Saemunan Church.
Schaefer, Donovan O. 2015. *Religious Affects: Animality, Evolution, and Power*. Durham, NC: Duke University Press.
Schipper, Kristofer and Franciscus Verellen, eds. 2004. *Taoist Canon*, vol 2. Chicago, IL: University of Chicago Press.
Schopen, Gregory. 1991. *Bones, Stones, and Buddhist Monks: Collected Papers on the Archaeology, Epigraphy, and Texts of Monastic Buddhism in India*. Honolulu: University of Hawaii Press. (Reprinted 1997)
———. 1975. "The Phrase '*prthivipradesas caityabhuto bhavet*' in the *Vajracchedika*: Notes on the Cult of the Book in Mahayana." *Indo-Iranian Journal* 17: 147–181.
Seckel, Dietrich. 1968 [1964]. *The Art of Buddhism*. Translated by Ann E. Keep. New York: Greystone Press.
Seo, Daeseok. 1991. "Dokgyeongsinang" (faith in reciting scriptures). In *Han-guk Minjok Munhwa Daebaekgwa* [Encyclopedia of Korean Culture]. Internet edition. http://encykorea.aks.ac.kr/Contents/Index?contents_id=E0015943. Accessed 25 July 2017.
Smart, Ninian. 2000. *World Views: Crosscultural Explorations of Human Beliefs*, 3rd ed. Upper Saddle River, NJ: Prentice-Hall.
Smith, Jonathan Z. 1987. *To Take Place: Toward Theory in Ritual*. Chicago, IL: University of Chicago Press.
———. 1990. *Drudgery Divine: On the Comparison of Early Christianities and the Religions of Late Antiquity*. Chicago, IL: University of Chicago Press.
———. 2000. "Epilogue: The 'End' of Comparison: Redescription and Rectification." In *A Magic Still Dwells: Comparative Religion in the Postmodern Age*, edited by Kimberley C. Patton and Benjamin C. Ray. Berkeley: University of California Press, 237-241.
———. 2004. *Relating Religion: Essays in the Study of Religion*. Chicago, IL: University of Chicago Press.
Smith, Wilfred Cantwell. 1971. "The Study of Religion and the Study of the Bible." *Journal of the American Academy of Religion* 39: 131–140. Reprinted 1989 in *Rethinking Scripture: Essays from a Comparative Perspective*, edited by Miriam Levering, 18–28. Albany: State University of New York Press.

———. 1989. "Scripture as Form and Concept: Their Emergence for the Western World." In *Rethinking Scripture: Essays from a Comparative Perspective*, edited by Miriam Levering, 29–57. Albany: State University of New York Press.

Song, Jubok. 1999. *Chuja Seodangeun Eotteoke Geureul Baewonna* [How master Chu school studied: translation and annotation of "On Reading," Chapter 10 and 11 of *Classified Conversations of Master Chu (Chu-tzu yü-lei)*]. Seongnam: Cheonggye.

Sperber, Dan. 1996. *Explaining Culture: A Naturalistic Approach*. Oxford: Blackwell Publishers.

Statistics Korea. 2016. *2015 Population and Housing Census Report*. http://kosis.kr/statisticsList/statisticsListIndex.do?menuId=M_01_01&vwcd=MT_ZTITLE&parmTabId=M_01_01#SelectStatsBoxDiv. Accessed 28 March, 2023.

Stoller, Pall and Cheryl Olkes. 1987. *In Sorcery's Shadow: A Memoir of Apprenticeship among the Songhay of Niger*. Chicago, IL: University of Chicago Press.

Strong, John S. 2002. *The Experience of Buddhism: Sources and Interpretation*. Belmont: Wadsworth/Thomson Learning.

Taylor, Rodney L. 1990. *The Religious Dimensions of Confucianism*. Albany: State University of New York Press.

The National Museum of Korea. 1991. *Bulsarijangeom* [*The Art of Sarira Reliquary*]. Seoul: The National Museum of Korea.

The Korea Mission Field. 1905–1907. Seoul

Tuladhar-Douglas, Will. 2009. "Writing and the Rise of Mahayana Buddhism." In *Die Texutalisierung der Religion*, edited by Joachim Schaper, 250–272. Tübingen: Mohr Siebeck.

Turner, Edith. 1992. *Experiencing Ritual: A New Interpretation of African Healing*. Philadelphia: University of Pennsylvania Press.

Turner, Victor. 1969. *The Ritual Process: Structure and Anti-Structure*. Chicago, IL: Aldine Publishing Company.

Vásquez, Manuel A. 2011. *More than Belief: A Materialist Theory of Religion*. Oxford: Oxford University Press.

Waghorne, Joanne Punzo. 2004. "Moving comparison out of the Scholars Laboratory." *Method & Theory in the Study of Religion* 16(1): 72–79.

———. 2010 [2012]. "A Birthday Party for a Sacred Text: The Gita Jayanti and the Embodiment of God as the Book and the Book as God," *Postscripts* 6: 225–242 [Reprinted in *Iconic Books and Texts*, edited by James W. Watts, 283–298. Sheffield: Equinox, 2013]

Watts, James W. 1999. *Reading Law: The Rhetorical Shaping of the Pentateuch*. Sheffield: Sheffield Academic Press.

———. 2006 [2008]. "The Three Dimensions of Scriptures." *Postscripts* 2: 135–159. [Reprinted in *Iconic Books and Texts*, edited by James W. Watts, 9–32. Sheffield: Equinox, 2013]

———. 2017. *Understanding the Pentateuch as a Scripture*. Oxford: Wiley-Blackwell.

———. 2019. *How and Why Books Matter: Essays on the Social Function of Iconic Texts*.

Bibliography

Sheffield: Equinox.
Watts, James W. and Yohan Yoo, eds. 2021. *Books as Bodies and as Sacred Beings.* Sheffield: Equinox.
Willemen, Charles. "Dharma and Dharmas." In *Encyclopedia of Buddhism.* vol. 1, edited by Robert E. Buswell Jr., 217–224. New York: Thomson Gale.
Williams, Paul. 2000. *Buddhist Thought.* New York: Routledge.
Wimbush, Vincent L. 2012. *White Men's Magic: Scripturalization as Slavery.* Oxford: Oxford University Press.
Yamabe, Nobuyoshi. 1999. "The Sutra on the Ocean-Like Samadhi of the Visualization of the Buddha." Unpublished Ph.D. thesis, Yale University.
Yesugyohoebo (Jesus Church Messenger Newspaper). 1912–1914. Seoul.
Yi, Deok-Ju. 1995. *Chogi Hanguk Gidokgyosa Yeongu* [A study on the early Christian history in Korea]. Seoul: The Institute for Korean Church History.
———. 2001. *Hanguk Tochakgyohoe Hyeongseongsa Yeongu* [A study on the formation of the indigenous church in Korea, 1903–1907]. Seoul: The Institute for the Korean Church History.
Yi, Hwang. (1568) 2009. *Seonghaksiptto* [*The Ten Diagrams on Sage Learning*]. Translated from Classical Chinese and Annotated by RIKS (Research Institute of Korean Studies, Korea University). Seoul: Sangjisa.
———. 2010. *Yijasueo* [*Essential Words of Master Yi*]. Edited by Yi Ik and An Jeongbok in 1753. Translated from Classical Chinse by Lee Gwangho. Seoul: Sangjisa.
Yi, Neunghwa. 1989 [1959]. *Joseon Dogyosa.* Seoul: Boseongmunhwasa.
Yi, Seonyong. 2016. "Urinara Bulbokjang-ui Teukjing" [Characteristics of Korean *bulbokang*]. *Korean Journal of Art History* 289: 93–119.
Yoo, Yohan. 2010 [2012]. "Possession and Repetition: Ways in Which Korean Lay Buddhists Appropriate Scriptures." *Postscripts* 6: 243–259.
———. 2019. "Performing Scriptures: Ritualizing Written Texts in *Seolwi-seolgyeong*, the Korean Shamanistic Recitation of Scriptures." *Postscripts* 10(1–2): 9–25.
———. 2023. "Material God Mengdu: A Symbol and Real Presence." In *Routledge Handbook of Material Religion*, edited by Pooyan Tamimi Arab, Jennifer Scheper Hughes, and S. Brent Rodríguez-Plate, 205-215. New York: Routledge.
Yun, Seoksan. 2009. "Suun Daesinsa-wa Donghak Cheondogyo, geurigo Donghak Gyeongjeon" [The Great Sacred Teacher Suun, Donghak Cheondogyo, and Donghak scriptures]. In *Juhae Donghakgyeongjeon: Donggyeongdaejeon/Yongdamyusa*, by Jeu Choe, 2009 (1880, 1881), 5–15. Seoul: Donghaksa.
———. 2014. "*Donggyeongdaejeon* Haeseol" [A commentary on *Donggyeongdaejeon*]. In *Donggyeongdaejeon*, Jeu Choe, 2014 [1880], 149–167. Seoul: Mosineunsaramdeul.
Yun, Seoksan and Seongyeop Hong. 2016. *Gyeongjeon-euro Bon Segyejonggyo: Cheondogyo* [World religions seen in scriptures: Cheondogyo]. Seoul: Jeontongmunhwayeonguhoe.

Korean Religious Texts in Iconic and Performative Rituals

Zuesse, Evan M. 2005. "Ritual." In *Encyclopedia of Religion,* 2nd Edition, edited by Lindsay Jones, 7833–7856. Farmington Hills, MI: Thompson Gale.

Index

A
affect, Affect theory 10–15, 18–21
An, Hyang 63
An, Sanggyeong 73–76, 80
ancestral rites 2, 120
ancient 5, 23, 55, 57, 59–60, 62, 68, 111
animality 10, 13–14, 19
anjeungut 72–74, 76, 79–80
antaekgut 73–74
Austin, J. L. 9, 22–23, 45, 49–50, 52–55, 57

B
Bai, Ju Yi 35
Bell, Catherine 7, 55, 71
beopsa see gyeonggaek
Bible vii, 9–12, 22–23, 30, 43–52, 54–57, 60
  Corinthians 54
  Epistles of Paul 47
  First Epistle of John 47
  Four Gospels 47
  Hebrew 51
  John 51, 54
  Leviticus vii
  Nehemiah 57
  Psalm 51
bokjang 88
Bosingyeong 73
Brown, C. Mackenzie 33–34, 106
bupbosi 40, 42

Buddha viii, 17, 20, 24, 27–28, 34–37, 38, 40–41, 61, 75–76, 83, 86–90, 92, 93, 94–95, 97–98
Buddha's belly viii, 86, 88–89
Buddhism, Buddhist viii, 1–3, 5, 20–22, 24, 27–30, 32–42, 48, 57, 60–61, 74–76, 78, 81, 85–90, 92, 93, 94–95, 97–98, 100, 102, 118–119
Bujeonggyeong 73
byeonggut 74, 80

C
Cabezón, José Ignacio 87, 95
Catholics, Catholicism 49, 100, 111, 119–120
Cheondogyo 100–101, 103, 105, 107, 113, 115–116, 122
Cheonjipalyanggyeong, Cheonjipalyangsinjugyeong 74–76
Cheonjon 74–76
China, Chinese x, 21, 23–25, 33, 35, 37, 41, 47, 59–60, 62–63, 66, 68, 75, 78, 80, 85, 88–90, 99–100, 102–104, 106–107, 109, 111–114, 117–118, 121–123
Ching, Julia 60–61
Christian, Christianity 2–5, 10, 12, 21–23, 43–52, 54–57, 60, 71, 107, 111
Cho, Dongil 119
Cho, Hyeonbum 100
Choe, Jeu 25, 100, 108–109, 111–116, 118–120
  Suun 100–122

Choe, Sihyeong 100, 102, 107–108, 114–117
  Haewol 100, 102, 107, 110, 114, 116–117, 119, 122
Choi, Geunyeong 28
Choi, Jongseong x, 99–101, 103–104, 108, 111, 113, 115–116
Chou 60
Chungcheong Province 4, 8, 69–70, 72–73, 78–79, 81
Chu, Hsi viii, 23, 60–68
Clark, A. D. 47
Collected Works of Master Chu 63–64, 67
comparative
  (study of) religion vii, 4–5, 21, 30, 51, 56
  research vii, 1
  perspective 2, 22, 31–32, 43–44, 56
comparison 4, 7, 21, 25, 44, 49, 54, 56–57, 61, 90, 104
Confucian, Confucianism x, 1–3, 5, 20–21, 23, 48, 57, 59–65, 67–68, 73, 75–76, 100, 102, 107, 116, 118, 121
  Neo-Confucian, Neo-Confucianism viii, 23, 59–65, 67–68
Confucius 59, 61, 63–64
contemplation 62, 68
cosmology 24, 72, 75, 81, 83, 109

D

Dallapiccola, A. L. 87
Daoism 61, 75–76, 100
darchor 35
death 37, 86, 102, 105, 107, 117
De Semini, Florinda 34
Deuchler, Martina 63
Devī Bhāgavata Purāṇa 106
devil 114–115, 117
dharani 29, 34–35, 37, 41–42, 87–89, 94
dharma 24, 27, 33–34, 81, 86–87, 89, 94, 97–98
divination 2, 31–32
dokgyeong 70, 72
Donggyeongdaejeon 24, 99, 101–111, 113–118, 121–123
  Gangsi 114
  Nonhakmun 103, 109
  Podeokmun 103, 108
  Sudeokmun 103, 109
Donghak ix–x, 2, 21, 24–25, 99–102, 104–111, *112*, 113–122
Donghakhakhoe 101–102, 110–111, 113, 119, 121
dongto 74
Doniger, Wendy 5, 25–26
Dosusa 108–109
Dupré, Louis 28

E

Eliade, Mircea 2–3, 16, 38, 40, 52, 60–61
Esposito, John L. 94–95
eumbo 119
evil 20, 23–24, 32, 38, 71–72, 74–76, 78–81, 83, 95, 97–98, 114

F

Fasching, Darrell J. 94–95
feeling 10–13, 16, 52–53, 61, 110, 120
Five Classics 59, 62–63
  Book of Rites 61
Four Books 60, 62–63, 67
  Analects 61

G

Gaeseong 27
Gagugyeonghaeng (Gyeonghaeng) 17, 27–28
Gardner, Daniel K. 61, 64–65
gasa x, 25, 99, 104–105, 118–119, 121–122
Geertz, Clifford 16, 28
Gethin, Rupert 28
Geum, Jangtae 63–65, 67
Gombrich, Richard 29, 34
Goodall, Jane 13, 18
Goryeo 27–28, 36, 63, 88, 118
Graham, William A. viii, 28–29, 31–33, 44, 49, 57, 59, 95
Great Revival 22, 43, 46, 56
Gregory, Peter N. 61
Gu, Junghoe 72, 75–76 78
gut 72–73, 78
gyeonggaek, gyeongjaengi 69–71, 73–74, 77, 78–81

Gyeongsang Province 103, 108, 114
Gyeongsangbukdo Province 35
Gyeongsangnamdo Province 37

H

Haeindo 37–38
Haeinsa temple *see* Haeindo
hanalnim 100, 103, 111
hangeul 102, 118
Han, Jeongdeok 79
Harari, Yuval Noah 14–15
Hardie, R. A. 46
Harvey, B. Peter 28
Hennessey, Anna Madelyn 61
holy 33, 46, 56, 59, 103, 106
Hong, Seongyeop 99–100, 102, 108, 110–111, 113–117
Hume, David 13
Hyegeun (Naong) 118

I

iconicity 85–87, 94, 98
Im, Seungbeom 72–73, 75, 81
Im, Taehong 111
incantation 21, 24, 74–75, 78, 99–111, 113–123
India, Indian 2–3, 28, 33, 35, 37, 40, 86–88, 106
Iri Koy 53

J

Jang, Inseong 72, 76
Japan, Japanese 29, 32–33, 35, 73, 100, 102
Jay, Nancy vii, 10
Jeju Province 4, 9, 17, 70
Jeokjoam temple 116
Jeong, Hyejeong 107, 110–111
Jeong, Sunu 63
Jesus 51, 54
Jewish 57, 71
jinbeop 81
Jogyesa temple 89
Johnson, Willard L. 28
Jones, Linsey 61
Joseon 2, 20, 27, 73, 75–76, 88, 102–103, 107–108, 118

Joseonwangjosillok 108
Ju, Gyeong-mi 88, 92
jumun 24, 103, 108, 110
  Bonjumun 107–108, 113–114, 118
  Chohakjumun 107–108
  Gangryeongjumun 107–108
  Jejajumun 107–108
  Seonsaengjumun 107

K

Kalton, Michael C. 63
karma 35, 37–38, 95
Kathmandu Valley 34
Kim, Chongsuh x
Kim, Gwangsu 45–48
Kim, Hyejeong 73–75, 80
Kim, Insu 46–47
Kim, Yeonjin 73–75, 80
Kim, Yonghwi 113
Kinnard, Jacob N. 33
KOSIS 102
Kugel, James L. 76
Küng, Hans 60

L

Levering, Miriam 31–34, 37, 40, 95
Lewis, Todd T. 94–95
Lim, Booyeon x
lips *see* mouth
Lofton, Kathryn ix
lun ts'ung 35
lungta 35

M

Mahayana 28–29, 33–35, 87
mandala 94
mantra 22, 29–30, 34–35, 37, 39, 41–42, 87, 94, 106
  Cundi Mantra 88
  Surangama Mantra 92
Marx, Karl 16
material 10–12, 17, 19–21, 28, 39, 72, 80, 87, 94–95
materialism 16
materiality 14, 19, 33
materialist 15–16, 19
materialistic vii, 10

materialize, materialization 4, 8, 15, 23–24, 34, 70–72, 76, 78–83
McMahan, David L. 61
Mencius 63
mengdu 17
metaphor 17, 61, 66–68
Meyer, Birgit 19
Min, Gyungbae 46, 56
mini-sutras 89–90, *91* miniature sutras viii, 24, 85–86, 88–90, *91*, 92, *93–94*, 95, *96*, 97–98
bokjangyong miniature sutras 95
hosinyong miniature sutras *94*, 95, 97
missionary 43, 45–49
Mitchell, Donald W. 28
modern 3–5, 16–17, 22, 24, 29
Moerman, D. Max 33
Moffett, Samuel Hugh 43–44, 46–47
Mongol, Mongolian 27, 36
monks 27–29, 33–35, 37, 39–40, 81, 92, 95, 102, 118
Moore, J. Z. 48
Moore, S. F. 46–47
Morgan, David 19, 62, 68
mouth 23, 51, 60, 62, 65, 68, 120
mudang, musogin 69, 73
Mun, Myeongdae 88
Muslims 49, 105
myth 15, 24, 52–53, 56, 105

N

Ndebbi 52
Ndembu 52–53
Nevius, John L. 47
new religious movement 2–3, 100, 107, 119

O

Oh, Munseon 78, 80–81
Okchugyeong 74–76, 80–81
Olkes, Cheryl 52
Orsi, Robert A. 17
Otto, Rudolf 13, 18

P

pagodas 87–89, 92
Paine, Crispin 19

Pak, Inho 116
palanquin 7, 17, 27
Pali 33
paper banner and figures 8–9, 20, 23–24, 70–72, 74, 77, 79–81, 83
Park, Byoung Hoon x, 103, 115–116, 119
Park, Hyejung 73–75, 80
Park, Jeongho 88
Park, Jong-ik 78, 81
Parmenter, Dorina Miller vii–viii, 10–12
pastors 43, 47–48, 50, 54
Patton, C. Kimberley 79
Patton, Laurie viii
Pentecostal 43, 46–47
performance, performing 7–10, 49, 54, 56, 70–71, 74, 78–79, 83, 86, 92, 94–95, 98, 105, 115–117, 122–123
performative vii–viii, x, 1–10, 12, 20, 22–23, 25–26, 44–45, 49–58, 70–71, 85, 90, 92, 95, 99, 105, 116–117, 121, 123
Peters, F. E. 71
Plate, Brent S. vii, 19, 60
Poole, F. J. P. 44
possession viii, 22, 27, 30, 34, 36–37, 40–42, 83, 85
Pratityasamutpadagatha 88
pre-modern 1, 3, 30
profane 7, 38, 40
Protestantism, Protestants 1, 4, 9–11, 20–22, 28, 43–50, 54–57
purify, purification 35, 39, 73–74
Pyeong-An Province 46
Pyongyang 46, 48, 54

Q

Qur'an 49

R

Rappaport, Roy 23, 55–57
Ray, Benjamin Caleb. 52–54
realms 73, 76, 110
relics 27, 29, 34–35, 87–88, 92
repetition viii, 22, 24, 27, 29–30, 34–37, 40, 42, 47, 97

Index

Rhi, Juhyung x, 88
Ricoeur, Paul 85
rinzo 35
rituals viii, 1–9, 17, 20–21, 23–25, 27–29, 32–38, 43–45, 47–58, 61, 70–74, 76, 78–81, 83, 86, 92, 94–95, 97–98, 104–105, 107, 115, 122
 African healing rituals 4, 9, 45, 52–54, 57
 burial rituals 33
 ritualize, ritualization viii, 1, 3, 5, 7–10, 12, 14, 17–18, 20–21, 23–26, 45, 49, 51, 55–57, 69–72, 76, 81, 83, 85, 99, 106, 115–117, 121–123
Robinson, Richard H. 28
rotating sutra 35, 37, 85

S

sages 59–65, 67–68
sagwi 74
sahada 105
sangje 111
Sanskrit 29, 33–34
sariras 87
Schaefer, Donovan O. 10, 12–15, 18–19
Schipper, Kristofer 75
Schleiermacher, Friedrich 13
Schopen, Gregory 28–29, 35
Scranton, William B. 45
SCRIPT vii–x, 1, 5–6, 10, 14, 21, 25
scripture vii–ix, 1–2, 4–12, 14, 18, 20–35, 38, 42–51, 54–65, 67–76, 77, 78–81, *82*, 83, 85–90, 92, 94–95, 97–111, 113–114, 117–122
Seckel, Dietrich 86–87
Seo, Daeseok 78
Seolwi-Seolgyeong viii, 8, 23–24, 69–72, 75–76, 78–80, 83
 seolwis 71–72, 77, 80–81, *82*
Seung-Dong Church 47
Shaman, Shamanism viii, 1–5, 8–9, 17, 20–21, 23–24, 60, 69–76, 78–81, 83
Sicheongyo *112*
Sicheonju 25, 107–108, 112–113
Silsangsa temple 88
simbang 17
Smart, Ninian 16, 55

Smith, Jonathan Z. 5–6, 13, 21, 44, 54, 56–57
Smith, Wilfred Cantwell 1, 22, 29–33, 42, 44, 59
Smith, William Robertson vii
Son, Byeonghui 100, 116
Songgwangsa temple 39
Songhay 52–53
Sperber, Dan 11
statue 24, 40, 86, 88–89, 92, *93*, 94–95, 98
Stoller, Paul 52–53
Strong, John S. 28
stupas 27, 87–88, 92
Sung 35, 62–63
susimjeonggi 114
Sutras 17, 22, 24, 27–30, 32–42, 60–61, 76, 86–87, 88–90, 92, 94–95, 97
 Avalokitesvara Sutra 90, 92, 97
 Benign King Prajna Sutra 17, 28
 Dhammapada 90
 Diamond Sutra 88–90, 92, 97
 Flower Ornament Sutra 37, 88–90, 92, 97
 Golden Light Sutra 89
 Great Dharani Sutra of Immaculate and Pure Light 88, 92
 Heart Sutra 41, 90, 92, 97
 Kstigarbha Sutra 89
 Lotus Sutra 89–90, 92, 97
 Mahaprajnaparamita Sutra 88
 Nirvana Sutra 86
 Prajnaparamita Sutra 34
 Surangama Sutra 89
 The Sutra of the Medicine Buddha's Vows 90
 Thousand Hands Sutra 41, 90, 92, 97
symbol 8, 17, 28, 32, 76, 110

T

Taiwan, Taiwanese 32–34, 95
talisman 33, 75, 95, 98, 105–106
Tang 35
Tan-huh 40
taste 23, 60–62, 65–68
Taylor, Rodney L. 59–60
Ten Diagrams on Sage Learning 63–64
The National Museum of Korea 88

139

Tibet, Tibetan 29, 35, 38
Toesingyeong 74
Tongdosa temple 39
tongues *see* mouth
Tripitaka 27, 36
Tuladhar-Douglas, Will 29, 34–37
Turner, Edith 52–53
Turner, Victor 52

U

Underwood, Horace G. 45

V

Vásquez, Manuel A. 15–16, 19
Verellen, Franciscus 75

W

Waghorne, Joanne Punzo 16, 34
Watts, James W. vii–viii, 1, 6–10, 25, 45, 49, 54, 57, 59, 71, 76, 79, 83, 85–86, 106, 119
Wesley, John 44
Willemen, Charles 87, 94
Williams, Paul 28
Wimbush, Vincent viii, 76, 110
Wonsan 46
worldview 2, 16, 69

Y

Yamabe, Nobuyoshi 61
Yeonboboyu 64
Yi, Deok-Ju 43, 48–49
Yi, Hwang viii, 23, 60–65, 67–68
Yi, Neunghwa 72
Yi, Seonyong 89
Yongdamyusa 24–25, 99, 101–105, 108–111, 115–116, 118–122
  Dodeokga 119
  Gyohunga 109, 119
  Heungbiga 109, 118
Yongmunsa temple *see yunjangdae*
Yoo, Yohan viii, 8–9, 17, 59, 78, 83, 106
yunjangdae 35, 36
Yun, Seoksan 99–100, 102, 108–111, 113–117
Yun, Woncheol viii–x
Yun, Yiheum 18–19

Z

Zuesse, Evan M. 6

Milton Keynes UK
Ingram Content Group UK Ltd.
UKHW021316241124
451398UK00001BA/9